Sonnets of Shakes

Mohan Vaishnav

[Author of *All & Everything in Diagrams*]

1

Published by   Shambhabi - The Third Eye Imprint,
                  A 10/ 1, Amarabati,
                  Sodepur, Kolkata – 700110
                  India

Price: INR Three hundred and twenty five only (Rs. 325/- only)

Dedication

I strived to know, of what psyche I'm made,
From where suddenly unfolds this or that trait
And without my knowing, I'm afraid,
Shapes my day-to-day life, and thus my fate?

I craved to mend my earthy home's every side,
But wasn't able to break free from my dome;
This agony, and often having rough ride
Showed the cunning of that insidious worm.

Haply, then, from the blues a herald came,
"Thou art wholly mine, so, here what's not mine?"
Which rested my heart in a sweet silent rhyme,
Making within the space for thy delight's rain.

O divine, let me dwell ever in this abode,
So, my eyes can kiss thy wealth on any road.

Acknowledgements

He wonders, in his life what's the place of verse?
Even in his furious or pensive state,
It does place his bosom beyond the purse
when he writes or reads, touching his soul straight.

He won't forget the help he has received
From foes, friends, teachers and the Heaven.
He thanks Life for all this for him it has conceived
And for the poise, to his Work, it has given.

But, how would he ever be able to thank thee
Sufficiently enough for thy eye's influence
Which helps him always wherever he might be?
Humbled, melted, he just stands in still silence!

Who could gift such a wondrous wealth to him?
It's thy, Sphinx-like, taintless eye's magic seem!

Table of Contents

29	When, in disgrace with fortune and men's eyes
30	When to the sessions of sweet silent thought
31	Thy bosom is endeared with all hearts
32	If thou survive my well-contented day
33	Full many a glorious morning have I seen
34	Why didst thou promise such a beauteous day
35	No more be griev'd at that which thou hast done
36	Let me confess that we two must be twain
37	As a decrepit father takes delight
38	How can my muse want subject to invent
39	O, how thy worth with manners may I sing
40	Take all my loves, my love, yea, take them all
41	Those petty wrongs that liberty commits
42	That thou hast her, it is not all my grief
43	When most I wink, then do mine eyes best see
44	If the dull substance of my flesh were thought
45	The other two, slight air and purging fire
46	Mine eye and heart are at a mortal war
47	Betwixt mine eye and heart a league is took
48	How careful was I when I took my way
49	Against that time, if ever that time come
50	How heavy do I journey on the way
51	Thus can my love excuse the slow offence
52	So am I as the rich, whose blessed key
53	What is your substance, whereof are you made
54	O, how much more doth beauty beauteous seem
55	Not marble, nor the gilded monuments
56	Sweet love, renew thy force; be it not said
57	Being your slave, what should I do but tend
58	That god forbid, that made me first your slave
59	If there be nothing new, but that which is
60	Like as the waves make towards the pebbled shore
61	Is it thy will thy image should keep open

62	Sin of self-love possesseth all mine eye
63	Against my love shall be, as I am now
64	When I have seen by time's fell hand defac'd
65	Since brass, nor stone, nor earth, nor boundless sea
66	Tir'd with all these, for restful death I cry
67	Ah, wherefore with infection should he live
68	Thus is his cheek the map of days outworn
69	Those parts of thee that the world's eye doth view
70	That thou art blamed shall not be thy defect
71	No longer mourn for me when I am dead
72	O, lest the world should task you to recite
73	That time of year thou mayest in me behold
74	But be contented: when that fell arrest
75	So are you to my thoughts, as food to life
76	Why is my verse so barren of new pride
77	Thy glass will show thee how thy beauties wear
78	So oft have I invoked thee for my muse
79	Whilst I alone did call upon thy aid
80	O, how I faint when I of you do write
81	Or I shall live your epitaph to make
82	I grant thou wert not married to my muse
83	I never saw that you did painting need
84	Who is it that says most? Which can say more
85	My tongue-tied muse in manners holds her still
86	Was it the proud full sail of his great verse
87	Farewell! Thou art too dear for my possessing
88	When thou shalt be dispos'd to set me light
89	Say that thou didst forsake me for some fault
90	Then hate me when thou wilt; if ever, now
91	Some glory in their birth, some in their skill
92	But do thy worst to steal thy self away
93	So shall I live, supposing thou art true
94	They that have power to hurt, and will do none

95	How sweet and lovely dost thou make the shame
96	Some say thy fault is youth, some wantonness
97	How like a winter hath my absence been
98	From you have I been absent in the spring
99	The forward violet thus did I chide
100	Where art thou, Muse, that thou forgett'st so long
101	O truant Muse, what shall be thy amends
102	My love is strengthen'd, though more weak in seeming
103	Alack! what poverty my Muse brings forth
104	To me, fair friend, you never can be old
105	Let not my love be call'd idolatry
106	When in the chronicle of wasted time
107	Not mine own fears, nor the prophetic soul
108	What's in the brain that ink may character
109	O, never say that I was false of heart
110	Alas, 'tis true, I have gone here and there
111	O, for my sake, do you with Fortune chide
112	Your love and pity doth the impression fill
113	Since I left you, mine eye is in my mind
114	Or whether doth my mind, being crown'd with you
115	Those lines that I before have writ, do lie
116	Let me not to the marriage of true minds
117	Accuse me thus; that I have scanted all
118	Like as, to make our appetites more keen
119	What potions have I drunk of Siren tears
120	That you were once unkind, befriends me now
121	'Tis better to be vile than vile esteemed
122	Thy gift, thy tables, are within my brain
123	No! Time, thou shalt not boast that I do change
124	If my dear love were but the child of state
125	Were it aught to me I bore the canopy
126	O thou, my lovely boy, who in thy power
127	In the old age black was not counted fair

128 How oft, when thou, my music, music play'st
129 The expense of spirit in a waste of shame
130 My Mistress' eyes are nothing like the sun
131 Thou art as tyrannous, so as thou art
132 Thine eyes I love, and they, as pitying me
133 Beshrew that heart that makes my heart to groan
134 So now I have confess'd that he is thine
135 Whoever hath her wish, thou hast thy will
136 If thy soul check thee that I come so near
137 Thou blind fool, Love, what dost thou to mine eyes
138 When my love swears that she is made of truth
139 O, call not me to justify the wrong
140 Be wise as thou art cruel; do not press
141 In faith I do not love thee with mine eyes
142 Love is my sin, and thy dear virtue hate
143 Lo, as a careful housewife runs to catch
144 Two loves I have of comfort and despair
145 Those lips that Love's own hand did make
146 Poor soul, the centre of my sinful earth
147 My love is as a fever, longing still
148 O me! what eyes hath love put in my head
149 Canst thou, O cruel! say I love thee not
150 O, from what power hast thou this powerful might
151 Love is too young to know what conscience is
152 In loving thee thou know'st I am forsworn
153 Cupid lay by his brand, and fell asleep
154 The little love-god, lying once asleep

Introduction

Deep understanding of human psyche, and the literary beauty & *meaning-density* of words, reflected in Works of William Shakespeare, is so beautiful & heart touching that, it makes it rank among the finest literature ever written, in any language.

The scope and subjects of Shakespeare's writing is enormously wide, he has encompassed almost every aspect of human psyche & human life in utmost depth. John Keats has said that Shakespeare lived a life of allegory, and his works are merely comments on it. For an awakened writer & poet like Shakespeare, to write Plays or Sonnets, it might not be necessary for him to personally undergo all those experiences in real life situations. It seems, his Muse has touched "Higher realms", unknown to ordinary human beings, to create such a literary beauty and psychologically so rich Sonnets, touching divinity through human love.

Since long there has been a scholarly dispute as to the identity of "the dark lady" and "the sweet boy" to whom many of Shakespeare's Sonnets are addressed, but, here, in this book, it is an attempt to briefly explain the meaning, depth and unwaveringness of love expressed in his Sonnets, without much bothering as to whom it is addressed. However, they have such a depth, precision and literary beauty that it is impossible to explain it fully; still this book is a humble attempt towards that aim.

Here it is interesting to note that many ancient male Indian sages and spiritual poets have written verses as female, addressing "the God", or "Higher Power", or "Invisible", as their Beloved.

This book intends to briefly explain the meaning of each Sonnet, so that the reading of original Sonnets become more enjoyable, even for a reader who may not be much familiar with Shakespearian style of writing.

Text or word written into brackets are either synonym of, or further explanation to, the preceding word or phrase.

Mohan Vaishnav
22nd June, 2014
Ahmedabad, India
mohan.vaishnav@gmail.com

Sonnet 1

From fairest creatures we desire increase,
That thereby beauty's rose might never die,
But as the riper should by time decease,
His tender heir might bear his memory:

But thou, contracted to thine own bright eyes,
Feed'st thy light's flame with self-substantial fuel,
Making a famine where abundance lies,
Thyself thy foe, to thy sweet self too cruel.

Thou that art now the world's fresh ornament,
And only herald to the gaudy spring,
Within thine own bud buriest thy content,
And, tender churl, makest waste in niggarding.

Pity the world, or else this glutton be,
To eat the world's due, by the grave and thee.

Explanation:

We desire that the most beautiful creatures of the nature bear its own off springs (growth), so that beauty's rose might never die; it is a general course of the nature that as any creature becomes ripe (aged), its tender heir (off spring) takes its place, and inherits the beauty of its predecessor.

But you, fascinated (contracted) to your own bright eyes, burning, like candle (wax), your own self to sustain your light's flame (beauty), making a famine where abundance lies (i.e. by neglecting to beget a child), you are proving your own enemy, and too cruel to your own sweet self.

You are now the world's fresh ornament, and the only one who perfectly represent the beauty & freshness of spring (only herald to the gaudy spring), but you are wasting such heavenly beauty in your utter greed (i.e. greed of sustaining physical beauty at the cost of begetting a child), and thereby burying the seed of beauty in your body itself.

Do mercy on this world (i.e. by begetting a child in whom your beauty will inherit, and will keep the world ornamented), otherwise, this (i.e. you not begetting a child) would mean, you are eating (destroying), like a glutton, not only the seed of beauty, but also yourself!

Sonnet 2

When forty winters shall besiege thy brow,
And dig deep trenches in thy beauty's field,
Thy youth's proud livery, so gazed on now,
Will be a tatter'd weed, of small worth held:

Then being ask'd where all thy beauty lies,
Where all the treasure of thy lusty days;
To say, within thine own deep-sunken eyes,
Were an all-eating shame and thriftless praise.

How much more praise deserved thy beauty's use,
If thou couldst answer – "This fair child of mine
Shall sum my count, and make my old excuse - "
Proving his beauty by succession thine!

This were to be new made when thou art old,
And see thy blood warm when thou feel'st it cold.

Explanation:

When you will be of 40 (when forty winters shall besiege your brow), and your age will reflect in beauty-spoiling wrinkles on your forehead, and your youth's present proud beauty, from which people are not able to take eyes off, will become like a worthless tattered weed.

That time people will ask, "Where all your beauty and the treasure of youthful lusty days lie?" Just think, how much shameful and worthless it would be for you to reply, "It lies in my own deep-sunken eyes"?

But, at that time, if you have child and you could reply "Sum of all my beauty lies (has succeeded) in this fair child of mine", then, how much more praise worthy your beauty's use would be!

When you are old your beauty will be new made in your child, and you will see your blood (i.e. your child) warm, even when the blood in your body feels cold.

Sonnet 3

Look in thy glass, and tell the face thou viewest
Now is the time that face should form another;
Whose fresh repair if now thou not renewest,
Thou dost beguile the world, unbless some mother.

For where is she so fair whose unear'd womb
Disdains the tillage of thy husbandry?
Or who is he so fond will be the tomb
Of his self-love, to stop posterity?

Thou art thy mother's glass, and she in thee
Calls back the lovely April of her prime:
So thou through windows of thine age shalt see,
Despite of wrinkles this thy golden time.

But if thou live, remember'd not to be,
Die single, and thine image dies with thee.

Explanation:

Look in the mirror and tell yourself that now is the time to beget a child (that face form another); if you not renew your face (by begetting a child), then, though you do charm the world by your beauty, it would mean you have unblessed some mother.

Because, can there be a beautiful lady who would hate to conceive a child in her unplowed fertile womb? Or can there be a man who would stop his posterity, and become the tomb of self-love?

In fact, now you are the mirror of your mother, and in you she calls back (sees) lovely April of her prime. In the same way, if you have child, in your old age you will see in him this your golden time.

But, if you live and die single without a child, your image and beauty will die with you, leaving you unremembered.

Sonnet 4

Unthrifty loveliness, why dost thou spend
Upon thyself thy beauty's legacy?
Nature's bequest gives nothing, but doth lend,
And, being frank, she lends to those are free.

Then, beauteous niggard, why dost thou abuse
The bounteous largess given thee to give?
Profitless usurer, why dost thou use
So great a sum of sums, yet canst not live?

For having traffic with thyself alone,
Thou of thyself thy sweet self dost deceive.
Then how, when nature calls thee to be gone,
What acceptable audit canst thou leave?

Thy unused beauty must be tomb'd with thee,
Which, used, lives th' executor to be.

Explanation:

Why are you carelessly spending your loveliness & inheritance of beauty upon yourself only? To be frank, I would say, the Nature gives nothing but it only lends, and it lends to those who are free giver.

Then, O beautiful greedy (beauteous niggard), why do you abuse such a generously bestowed gift (largess), which is given to you for onward giving? O profitless usurer (usurer is a person who lends money to people at unfairly high rates of interest), why do you use such a great sum of sums, and still be unable to live?

If you love yourself alone (have traffic with thyself alone), then you yourself are deceiving your sweet self (soul). And then how, when the Nature make you die (when nature calls thee to be gone), what worthy legacy would you leave behind (what acceptable audit canst thou leave)?

Your unused beauty will be buried (tombed) with you, but, if it is used (i.e. to beget a child), it will live immortalized in your heir.

Sonnet 5

Those hours that with gentle work did frame
The lovely gaze where every eye doth dwell,
Will play the tyrants to the very same,
And that unfair which fairly doth excel;

For never-resting time leads summer on
To hideous winter and confounds him there;
Sap check'd with frost, and lusty leaves quite gone,
Beauty o'ersnow'd, and bareness every where:

Then, were not summer's distillation left,
A liquid prisoner pent in walls of glass,
Beauty's effect with beauty were bereft,
Nor it, nor no remembrance what it was.

But flowers distill'd, though they with winter meet,
Leese but their show; their substance still lives sweet.

Explanation:

This very Time, which has so gently articulated the lovely gaze in your eyes, to which every one is fascinated to look at, will play the tyrant and will destroy that very same, and that unfair which fairly does excel;

Because, the never-resting time leads summer (good time) on to horrific winter (bad time), which makes the sap (nectar) of plants freeze with frost, and its lusty leaves dead, and that leaves the beauty of the Nature over-snowed, and so the bareness every where.

At that time, if the scent of summer's flowers were not distilled and bottled, then beauty's effect (i.e. perfume) also dies with beauty (i.e. flowers), and no one remembers that how beautifully sweet smelling they were!

But, the distilled flowers (flowers distilled into scent), though dies physically when they meet the winter, still the sweetness of their substance (perfume) lives on. (Therefore, you distill your beauty by begetting a child, or you distill your physical body to produce something higher in your being, so that it can live on for ever).

Sonnet 6

Then let not winter's ragged hand deface
In thee thy summer, ere thou be distill'd:
Make sweet some vial; treasure thou some place
With beauty's treasure, ere it be self-kill'd.

That use is not forbidden usury,
Which happies those that pay the willing loan;
That's for thyself to breed another thee,
Or ten times happier, be it ten for one;

Ten times thyself were happier than thou art,
If ten of thine ten times refigured thee:
Then what could Death do, if thou shouldst depart,
Leaving thee living in posterity?

Be not self-will'd, for thou art much too fair
To be Death's conquest and make worms thine heir.

Explanation:

Before Time's (winter's) ragged hand spoil your beauty in you (deface in thee thy summer), you be distilled (i.e. beget a child); make some phial (womb) sweet (pregnant); and treasure yourself at some place with your beauty's treasure (i.e. make womb pregnant and treasure your beauty's treasure in the child conceived therein), before your beauty be self-killed (by aging).

That usury (i.e. that practice of lending money to people at unfairly high rates of interest) is not forbidden in which the repayment of willing loan makes the borrowers happy; it is for you to breed yourself into another you (i.e. into an offspring), and if you do it for ten times (i.e. beget ten children), you will be ten times happier!

If each of your ten children replicates (refigure) you ten times (i.e. each beget ten children), you will be ten times happier than you are now. Then, what harm death could do to you, if you die leaving yourself living in posterity?

So, don't be so willful, because you are much too beauteous to be conquered by Death, and be merely consumed by worms on your childless death.

Sonnet 7

Lo, in the orient when the gracious light
Lifts up his burning head, each under eye
Doth homage to his new-appearing sight,
Serving with looks his sacred majesty;

And having climb'd the steep-up heavenly hill,
Resembling strong youth in his middle age,
Yet mortal looks adore his beauty still,
Attending on his golden pilgrimage;

But when from high-most pitch, with weary car,
Like feeble age, he reeleth from the day,
The eyes, 'fore duteous, now converted are
From his low tract, and look another way:

So thou, thyself outgoing in thy noon,
Unlook'd on diest, unless thou get a son.

Explanation:

In the east (orient) when the Sun (gracious light) rises (lifts up his burning head), every eye on the earth give homage to his new-appearing sight (as the Sun is new every morning), by giving humble look (serving with looks) to his sacred majesty.

And, eyes of the people (mortal looks) attending on to his golden pilgrimage, adore his beauty even still, as he like a strong youth in his prime age, moves up in the sky (steep-up heavenly hill).

But when the same Sun reels down, like a tired feeble aged man, from his peak (high-most pitch), eyes of the people, which were duteous before, are now converted from his low tract (path of coming down towards the setting), and looks elsewhere.

So are you, now at your youth's peak (outgoing in thy noon), but will not be so looked at in your old age, unless you beget a son.

Sonnet 8

Music to hear, why hear'st thou music sadly?
Sweets with sweets war not, joy delights in joy,
Why lovest thou that which thou receivest not gladly?
Or else receivest with pleasure thine annoy?

If the true concord of well-tuned sounds,
By unions married, do offend thine ear,
They do but sweetly chide thee, who confounds
In singleness the parts that thou shouldst bear.

Mark how one string, sweet husband to another,
Strikes each in each by mutual ordering;
Resembling sire and child and happy mother,
Who, all in one, one pleasing note do sing:

Whose speechless song, being many, seeming one,
Sings this to thee: "thou single wilt prove none."

Explanation:

When you are listening music, why you hear it sadly? Don't make the sweetness of music at war with the sweetness of your Self. Because, when joy giving thing is enjoyed while being in a better state, it gives more delight. Why do you love doing that thing which doesn't make you glad? Or else bear your annoyance with pleasure.

If the well-tuned sounds' unification into a perfect harmony offends your ear, then, know that they (i.e. constituent sounds of a harmony) sweetly rebuke you, who limits oneself into singleness, and do not beget children that you should beget (who confounds in singleness the parts that you should bear).

Just see, in a perfect harmony how one string (sound) is like sweet husband to another, and strike one another in mutual ordering like a lovely family of respected father, child and happy mother, who all together sing one pleasing note.

And whose speechless song, which are, in fact, many but sounds as one, says this to you: "being single (love-empty) you will prove to be none (worthless)."

Sonnet 9

Is it for fear to wet a widow's eye
That thou consum'st thyself in single life?
Ah! if thou issueless shalt hap to die.
The world will wail thee, like a makeless wife;

The world will be thy widow, and still weep
That thou no form of thee hast left behind,
When every private widow well may keep,
By children's eyes, her husband's shape in mind.

Look, what an unthrift in the world doth spend
Shifts but his place, for still the world enjoys it:
But beauty's waste hath in the world an end,
And kept unused, the user so destroys it.

No love toward others in that bosom sits,
That on himself such murderous shame commits.

Explanation:

Are you consuming yourself in single (love-empty) life because you fear that on your death someone would become a sad widow? But, if you happen to die childless, people will wail you like a childless wife.

Every individual widow may keep, by her children's eyes, her husband's face well alive in her mind, but on your death the whole world will be your widow, and will still weep that you have not left any of your form (Child or Soul) behind (to keep alive your face in it).

See, when unthrift person wastes his wealth, it goes in the hands of others and in that way the world still enjoys it, but, if the beauty is so wasted, it comes to an end, and is destroyed for ever.

Only he can commit such murderous shame on himself, in whose heart there is no love towards others.

Sonnet 10

For shame! deny that thou bear'st love to any,
Who for thyself art so unprovident.
Grant if thou wilt thou art beloved of many,
But that thou none lovest is most evident;

For thou art so possess'd with murderous hate,
That 'gainst thyself thou stick'st not to conspire,
Seeking that beauteous roof to ruinate,
Which to repair should be thy chief desire.

O, change thy thought, that I may change my mind!
Shall hate be fairer lodged than gentle love?
Be, as thy presence is, gracious and kind,
Or to thyself, at least, kind-hearted prove;

Make thee another self, for love of me,
That beauty still may live in thine or thee.

Explanation:

For shame's sake tell that you have no love for anyone. Oh, how careless you are for your own self! Confess, if you can, that you are the beloved of many, but you love none but yourself.

It should be your chief desire to keep your real beauty in good repair, but, on the contrary, you are so possessed with murderous hate that even you don't hesitate to conspire to ruin your that very beauty itself.

O, change your thoughts so that I change my mind about you! Do you think it shall be fairer to keep hate placed in the heart, rather than gentle love? Be, as your presence is, gracious and kind; otherwise at least prove kind-hearted to your own self.

For my love's sake, make yourself another self (i.e. beget a child or transform your self into Soul), so that your beauty may live in your children or in your Soul always.

Sonnet 11

As fast as thou shalt wane, so fast thou grow'st
In one of thine, from that which thou departest.
And that fresh blood which youngly thou bestow'st
Thou mayst call thine, when thou from youth convertest.

Herein lives wisdom, beauty, and increase:
Without this, folly, age, and cold decay:
If all were minded so, the times should cease,
And threescore year would make the world away.

Let those whom Nature hath not made for store,
Harsh, featureless, and rude, barrenly perish:
Look whom she best endow'd, she gave the more;
Which bounteous gift thou shouldst in bounty cherish;

She carved thee for her seal, and meant thereby
Thou shouldst print more, not let that copy die.

Explanation:

As fast as you are waning (aging), so fast you shall grow in your child; and the fresh blood which you bestow now to your child, shall be called yours when you shall become old aged.

In this only there lies wisdom, beauty and growth; otherwise, without this, there shall be foolishness, aging and cold decay. If all people think not to beget children, then within next 60 years or so, there shall be no one alive on this earth, and life & time shall end.

Let those harsh, beauty-less and rude ones, whom the Nature has not made for inheritance, perish barren and childless. Just see, whom the Nature endows its best, bestows it in abundance. You should cherish this bounteous gift (i.e. your beauty) the Nature has bestowed upon you, and should make for its inheritance.

The Nature has carved you as her seal, and thereby she meant that you should print more (i.e. beget children), and not let the copy of your beauty die.

Sonnet 12

When I do count the clock that tells the time,
And see the brave day sunk in hideous night;
When I behold the violet past prime,
And sable curls, all silver'd o'er with white;

When lofty trees I see barren of leaves,
Which erst from heat did canopy the herd,
And summer's green all girded up in sheaves,
Borne on the bier with white and bristly beard;

Then of thy beauty do I question make,
That thou among the wastes of time must go,
Since sweets and beauties do themselves forsake,
And die as fast as they see others grow;

And nothing 'gainst Time's scythe can make defence
Save breed, to brave him when he takes thee hence.

Explanation:

When I happen to count hours through the time-telling clock, and see that beautiful day passes into ugly night; when I reminisce the prime past that has gone, and see the dark beautiful curls (hairs) all converted into silvered white;

When I see the lofty (grand) trees which once did give shelter and shade, but are now barren of leaves, and see green grass all cut and bunched for carrying, and see some aged one being carried on coffin with white and bristly beard,

Then, about your beauty a question arises in my mind that you and your beauty, among other wastes of time must go, since all sweets and beauties forsake themselves and die as fast as they see others grow;

Nothing, other than the breed (i.e. child or all loving immortal Soul) can prove to be a defence against Time's scythe, to fight it when the death will knock your door.

Sonnet 13

O, that you were yourself! but, love, you are
No longer yours than you yourself here live:
Against this coming end you should prepare,
And your sweet semblance to some other give.

So should that beauty which you hold in lease
Find no determination: then you were
Yourself again, after yourself's decease,
When your sweet issue your sweet form should bear.

Who lets so fair a house fall to decay,
Which husbandry in honour might uphold
Against the stormy gusts of winter's day
And barren rage of death's eternal cold?

O, none but unthrifts! Dear my love, you know
You had a father; let your son say so.

Explanation:

How nice if your body were yours for ever, but, my beloved, your body is no longer yours than the period for which you are alive here. You should prepare yourself against this inevitable coming end (death) by begetting a child, and by giving your sweet semblance to him.

After your body's death (yourself's decrease) when your sweet child bear your sweet resemblance (form), you shall be yourself again (i.e. in your child), and your beauty which you hold in lease shall find no end (determination).

Who will uphold the honor of such husbandry which lets so beautiful a house to fall to decay, and makes it a victim of stormy gusts of winter's day and barren rage of death's eternal cold?

No one other than an utter unthrift can do so. My beloved, you know that you had a father; beget a son, so that he also can say, "I had a father".

Sonnet 14

Not from the stars do I my judgment pluck;
And yet methinks I have astronomy,
But not to tell of good or evil luck,
Of plagues, of dearths, or seasons' quality;

Nor can I fortune to brief minutes tell,
Pointing to each his thunder, rain, and wind,
Or say with princes if it shall go well,
By oft predict that I in heaven find:

But from thine eyes my knowledge I derive,
And (constant stars) in them I read such art,
As truth and beauty shall together thrive,
If from thyself to store thou wouldst convert;

Or else of thee this I prognosticate:
Thy end is truth's and beauty's doom and date.

Explanation:

I do not gather my judgment from the stars, still I think I have astronomy, but this is not for predicting about good or evil luck, or calamity, or famines, or season's quality;

Neither can I tell minute details of fortune pointing to each thunder, rain and wind, nor do I predict about good or bad luck of princes from the position and movements of planets.

But I derive my knowledge from your eyes. I read that in these your two constant unshakable stars there exist such an art that in them truth and beauty both shall together thrive, if you convert them from yourself to womb (i.e. if you beget a child).

Otherwise, about you I predict that: your death would be the death of truth and beauty itself !!!

Sonnet 15

When I consider every thing that grows
Holds in perfection but a little moment,
That this huge stage presenteth nought but shows
Whereon the stars in secret influence comment;

When I perceive that men as plants increase,
Cheered and check'd even by the self-same sky;
Vaunt in their youthful sap, at height decrease,
And wear their brave state out of memory;

Then the conceit of this inconstant stay
Sets you most rich in youth before my sight,
Where wasteful Time debateth with decay,
To change your day of youth to sullied night;

And, all in war with Time, for love of you,
As he takes from you, I engraft you new.

Explanation:

When I think that every thing that grows and stands in perfection but for a little moment only, and that on this huge world-stage everything that happens is a mere Play controlled by the secret influent of stars and planets;

When I perceive that just like plants, men increase, become happy & unhappy by unknown heavenly influences, show off in their youthful days, starts decreasing from their peak, and loose the memory of higher state they achieved;

Then the Time's this very conceit of inconstant stay, wherein all eating Time changes your day of youth into sullied night by decaying you. But for me it makes you seem most rich in youth before my sight.

Moreover, all are in constant war with Time for love of you. As the Time takes away beauty from you (i.e. by aging you), I engraft you new with my increased love. (That is, in spite of your aging, to my heart's eyes, day by day, you seem more & more beautiful, such is my love!)

Sonnet 16

But wherefore do not you a mightier way
Make war upon this bloody tyrant, Time?
And fortify yourself in your decay
With means more blessed than my barren rhyme?

Now stand you on the top of happy hours;
And many maiden gardens, yet unset,
With virtuous wish would bear your living flowers,
Much liker than your painted counterfeit:

So should the lines of life that life repair,
Which this, Time's pencil, or my pupil pen,
Neither in inward worth, nor outward fair,
Can make you live yourself in eyes of men.

To give away yourself keeps yourself still;
And you must live, drawn by your own sweet skill.

Explanation:

Why are you not making war upon this bloody tyrant Time with a mightier way and fortify yourself in your decay, with means more blessed than this my barren lines?

Presently you are in the happiest phase of your life, and still many new gardens are yet to be set with your virtuous wish, bearing you living flowers (i.e. children) much more beauteous than your painted portrait.

In the same way, neither in your beauty's journey through the passage of your life time, nor in this my child-like lines have enough strength to make you live in eye of men for ever.

But, if you give away yourself in love and beget a child, you would live for ever, reflecting your shape, beauty and sweet skill in your posterity.

Sonnet 17

Who will believe my verse in time to come,
If it were fill'd with your most high deserts?
Though yet, Heaven knows, it is but as a tomb
Which hides your life, and shows not half your parts.

If I could write the beauty of your eyes,
And in fresh numbers number all your graces,
The age to come would say 'This poet lies:
Such heavenly touches ne'er touch'd earthly faces.'

So should my papers, yellow'd with their age,
Be scorn'd, like old men of less truth than tongue;
And your true rights be term'd a poet's rage,
And stretched metre of an antique song:

But were some child of yours alive that time,
You should live twice; - in it, and in my rhyme.

Explanation:

Who will believe my verse in time to come, if I write all your most superior qualities and beauty in it? Though yet, God knows that still it would be, merely like a tomb, which hides your life and can not shows even half of your qualities.

If I could write the beauty of your eyes, and count all your graces afresh (i.e. in my verses), the generation (age) to come would say "This poet lies: such heavenly beauty has never glowed upon human faces."

In the same way, my papers (on which my poetry about you has been written) yellowed with age over a period would be scorned like lying old men of less truth than tongue, and your true qualities would be taken as poet's (my) rage (passion), and much exaggerated praise of your beauty.

But if some child of yours were alive that time, then you would live twice: (1) in your child, as your beauty and grace would live on reflected in it and (2) in my poem, as it would be believed as true statement of your graces.

Sonnet 18

Shall I compare thee to a summer's day?
Thou art more lovely and more temperate:
Rough winds do shake the darling buds of May,
And summer's lease hath all too short a date:

Sometime too hot the eye of heaven shines,
And often is his gold complexion dimm'd;
And every fair from fair sometime declines,
By chance, or nature's changing course, untrimm'd;

But thy eternal summer shall not fade,
Nor lose possession of that fair thou owest;
Nor shall Death brag thou wander'st in his shade,
When in eternal lines to time thou growest;

So long as men can breathe, or eyes can see,
So long lives this, and this gives life to thee.

Explanation:

Should I compare you with a summer's day? (The summer is most beautiful & warm season in England). In fact, you are lovelier and more temperate than summer's day, as, many times in May rough winds do blow and shake beautiful budding flowers, and also the summer season time is very short.

In summer, sometimes the Sun is too hot, and sometimes its golden beauty is dimmed when the sky is clouded. As such, the beauty of every beautiful thing declines over a time, sometimes by chance, and sometimes by rule of nature.

But, your eternal youth shall never fade, and the beauty that you owe shall never decline, not even the death would make your wonder buried in his (i.e. death's) dark shade, as you & your beauty shall ever remain alive in my this eternal lines (rather, not only you shall live beautiful in my poem but my this timeless poem shall make you seem even more and more beautiful as the time pass by).

So long there live humanity on the Earth and human eye is able to see, this my timeless lines (poem) shall live, and shall keep you & your beauty alive in eyes of men.

Sonnet 19

Devouring Time, blunt thou the lion's paws,
And make the earth devour her own sweet brood;
Pluck the keen teeth from the fierce tiger's jaws,
And burn the long-lived phoenix in her blood;

Make glad and sorry seasons, as thou fleets,
And do whate'er thou wilt, swift-footed Time,
To the wide world, and all her fading sweets;
But I forbid thee one most heinous crime:

O, carve not with thy hours my love's fair brow,
Nor draw no lines there with thine antique pen;
Him in thy course untainted do allow,
For beauty's pattern to succeeding men.

Yet, do thy worst, old Time: despite thy wrong,
My love shall in my verse ever live young.

Explanation:

O all-eating Time, if you wish, you may blunt the lion's paws, and make the Earth eat her own sweet brood (offspring-produces), pluck the keen (sharp) teeth from the fierce tiger's jaws, and burn the long-lived phoenix in her blood (phoenix is a bird which burns itself and again become alive from its own ashes).

O sweet-footed (quickly fleeting) Time, you may make the good times & bad times to come & go during your journey, and do whatever you wish to this entire World, and to all its beautiful things, but, I forbid you to do one heinous crime (that is, I order you not to do the following heinous crime):

Never make my love's beautiful brow look aged, nor draw wrinkles on my love's forehead (i.e. by aging), and let him remain untainted (ever youthful, un-aged) all during your passage (for ever), so that the generations to come can see, how beautiful a man can be!

Yet, O old Time, do your worst (do whatever you wish to my beloved): despite the fact that you would age him, my love shall ever live (remain) young in this my timeless verse!

Sonnet 20

A woman's face, with Nature's own hand painted,
Hast thou, the master-mistress of my passion;
A woman's gentle heart, but not acquainted
With shifting change, as is false women's fashion;

An eye more bright than theirs, less false in rolling,
Gilding the object whereupon it gazeth;
A man in hue, all hues in his controlling,
Much steals men's eyes, and women's souls amazeth.

And for a woman wert thou first created;
Till Nature, as she wrought thee, fell a-doting,
And by addition me of thee defeated,
By adding one thing to my purpose nothing.

But since she prick'd thee out for women's pleasure,
Mine be thy love, and thy love's use their treasure.

Explanation:

O, you have the face of master mistress of my passion (face of the woman whom I love to love passionately), which the Nature has created so beautiful by its own hand. Though your heart is gentle like woman's heart, but your heart is not shifting & changing like false woman's fashion.

Your eye is brighter than eye of any woman, but (like woman's eye) it is not moving here & there (in inviting & evoking manner). That object becomes beautiful (gilded) upon which your eye gazes. Your appearance is such that it controls all's love & passion, and steals other men's eyes, but gives happiness to women's souls.

You were first created as woman, but seeing your unparallel beauty the Nature, who created you, herself fell in love with you so passionately that she turned you into man, and by that the Nature has made no good to me and made me defeated (in gaining your love).

But since the Nature has pricked you (i.e. made you a man) for women's pleasure, so let all your love be mine, and your love's use (i.e. your sex) be women's treasure.

Sonnet 21

So is it not with me as with that muse,
Stirr'd by a painted beauty to his verse;
Who heaven itself for ornament doth use,
And every fair with his fair doth rehearse;

Making a couplement of proud compare,
With sun and moon, with earth and sea's rich gems,
With April's first-born flowers, and all things rare
That heaven's air in this huge rondure hems.

O let me, true in love, but truly write,
And then believe me, my love is as fair
As any mother's child, though not so bright
As those gold candles fix'd in heaven's air:

Let them say more than like of hearsay well;
I will not praise, that purpose not to sell.

Explanation:

I am not like a poet who, inspired (stirred) to make his verse beautiful, ornament his beloved by equating his beloved with all beautiful things of the Nature.

Nor I will make a couplement (union), for proudly comparing the beloved, with sun & moon, with earth's & sea's rich gems, with April's first-born flowers and all rare things around the globe.

As I am true in love, so let me truly write, and then believe me, my love is as fair as any mother's child, though may not be so bright as the Stars (gold candles fixed in heaven's air).

Let other poets say well more like of hearsay (let other poets say well about something which is more like gossip rather than facts), but I will not praise you for that purpose (i.e. for false comparison's sake), nor will I praise to sell (i.e. to make it popular).

Sonnet 22

My glass shall not persuade me I am old,
So long as youth and thou are of one date;
But when in thee time's furrows I behold,
Then look I death my days should expiate.

For all that beauty that doth cover thee
Is but the seemly raiment of my heart,
Which in thy breast doth live, as thine in me:
How can I then be elder than thou art?

O therefore, love, be of thyself so wary,
As I not for myself but for thee will;
Bearing thy heart, which I will keep so chary
As tender nurse her babe from faring ill.

Presume not on thy heart when mine is slain;
Thou gavest me thine, not to give back again.

Explanation:

The mirror shall not persuade me that I am old, so long as you are young (so long as youth and you are of one date), but when I will see wrinkles (time's furrow – aging effects) in you, that would be the time of my death (that is, I would like to die rather than seeing time's furrow – wrinkles - aging effect in you).

Because all your beauty is but the clothing ornament (seemly raiment) of my heart, which lives in your breast, as your heart lives in mine (that is, my heart lives in your body and your heart lives in my body), so, how can I be elder than you are?

O my love, therefore, take utmost care of yourself, as I will take care of myself, not for myself, but for you, as your heart lives in my body, for which I am always so careful as like the tender nurse who is always so careful for keeping her baby away from illness.

But, do not presume on your heart (i.e. do not presume that your heart will remain unaffected) when my heart is dead, as once you gave me your heart, it was not meant for giving back again.

Sonnet 23

As an unperfect actor on the stage,
Who with his fear is put besides his part,
Or some fierce thing replete with too much rage,
Whose strength's abundance weakens his own heart;

So I, for fear of trust, forget to say
The perfect ceremony of love's rite,
And in mine own love's strength seem to decay,
O'ercharg'd with burden of mine own love's might.

O, let my books be, then, the eloquence
And dumb presagers of my speaking breast;
Who plead for love, and look for recompense
More than that tongue that more hath more express'd.

O, learn to read what silent love hath writ:
To hear with eyes belongs to love's fine wit.

Explanations:

As like an imperfect actor who is not able to perform on stage because of his fear, or, like some fierce thing full of rage, the abundance of whose strength itself has weakened its own existence.

So am I, for fear of trust, not able to express my love in words, as my love for you is so overcharged with its own intensity that it is not able to express itself.

So, instead of expressing my love in words, let the love-full-ness of my appearance itself be eloquent, and world-less presage (uneasiness) of my speaking breast itself, which is full of love for you and asks for your love in return, be the expression of my love.

O my love, learn to read (understand) what silent (unspoken) love has expressed, as, to hear with eyes (i.e. to discern the meaning just by looking at) is the capacity of fine (true & deep) love only.

Sonnet 24

Mine eye hath play'd the painter, and hath stell'd
Thy beauty's form in table of my heart;
My body is the frame wherein 'tis held,
And perspective it is the best painter's art.

For through the painter must you see his skill,
To find where your true image pictur'd lies,
Which in my bosom's shop is hanging still,
That hath his windows glazed with thine eyes.

Now see what good turns eyes for eyes have done:
Mine eyes have drawn thy shape, and thine for me
Are windows to my breast, where-through the sun
Delights to peep, to gaze therein on thee;

Yet eyes this cunning want to grace their art;
They draw but what they see, know not the heart.

Explanation:

My eye has drawn a painting of your beauty in my heart, and my body is the frame for that painting, and that painting has been drawn in the best perspective art (i.e. in a very realistic articulate manner).

Look at it with an artist's eye to see his (i.e. my eye's) skill of painting your true image that lies hanging still (unmoved) in my bosom's shop (heart), which has its windows gazed with your eyes.

Now see what mutual good the eye for eye have done; my eyes have drawn your painting, and your eyes, for me, are windows to my heart, through which the sun delights to peep (secretly look at) and gaze upon you there.

But still there is a cunning want (drawback) in this art; they (i.e. eyes) can draw painting of what they see, but know not the heart.

Sonnet 25

Let those who are in favour with their stars,
Of public honour and proud titles boast,
Whilst I, whom fortune of such triumph bars,
Unlook'd for joy in that I honour most.

Great princes' favourites their fair leaves spread
But as the marigold at the sun's eye,
And in themselves their pride lies buried,
For at a frown they in their glory die.

The painful warrior famoused for fight,
After a thousand victories once foil'd,
Is from the book of honour razed quite,
And all the rest forgot for which he toil'd:

Then happy I, that love and am beloved
Where I may not remove, nor be removed.

Explanation:

Let all those feel boasted, who are born under lucky stars making them fated to have public honor and proud titles. But I, who am not bestowed with such good luck, feel happy in unexpected joy that comes along.

All those, who are favorites of great princes, enjoy spread of their fair leaves (i.e. spread of fresh & new spheres of gratifications), but it is all like marigold (marigold is kind of a yellow flower which opens in day time and dies at evening), only under the favoring eye of their prince (boss); their pride gets buried in themselves and their glory dies just by a frown (unfavorable look) of their prince (boss).

The laborious warrior who is famous for his ability to fight, and who has a thousand victory under his fold, but when he gets defeated once, all his honor is wiped out and all his previous victories, for which he toiled all his life, is completely forgotten.

So, then, I am the happy one, who loves, and is being loved, and who never abandon his love, and is never abandoned by his love.

Sonnet 26

Lord of my love, to whom in vassalage
Thy merit hath my duty strongly knit,
To thee I send this written embassage,
To witness duty, not to show my wit.

Duty so great, which wit so poor as mine
May make seem bare, in wanting words to show it,
But that I hope some good conceit of thine
In thy soul's thought, all naked, will bestow it:

Till whatsoever star that guides my moving,
Points on me graciously with fair aspect,
And puts apparel on my tatter'd loving,
To show me worthy of thy sweet respect:

Then may I dare to boast how I do love thee,
Till then, not show my head where thou mayst prove me.

Explanation:

O lord of my love, your merit (virtues) has strongly bound me to serve you dutifully as vassal (servant); I send this written embassage (message) to you, just as token of my duty, and not to show my cleverness or poetic skill.

My duty towards you is so great, and my skill to fulfill it is so poor that it may appear bare & poorly worded, but I hope that your some good conceit (i.e. your generous forgiveness) arising from your soul's thought will bestow (accept) it;

Till the star (I don't know which one) that guides & influences my luck, cast its fair (good) aspect upon me and beautify my tattered (torn) love, and make me worthy of your sweet respect (love).

Then I would dare to boast how much I do love you, till then, I will not show my head, and will stand bow-headed.

Sonnet 27

Weary with toil, I haste me to my bed,
The dear repose for limbs with travel tired;
But then begins a journey in my head,
To work my mind, when body's work's expired:

For then my thoughts (from far where I abide)
Intend a zealous pilgrimage to thee,
And keep my drooping eyelids open wide,
Looking on darkness which the blind do see:

Save that my soul's imaginary sight
Presents thy shadow to my sightless view,
Which, like a jewel hung in ghastly night,
Makes black night beauteous, and her old face new.

Lo, thus, by day my limbs, by night my mind
For thee, and for myself, no quiet find.

Explanation:

Weary with toil, I haste myself to my bed to have dear repose (deep rest) for my travel tired limbs (body), but, then, as soon as the body's work is expired (i.e. as soon as the physical work is over), journey begins in my head by the working of the mind (i.e. by flow of thoughts in mind).

That time (i.e. at night) my thoughts, from far where I abide (reside) intend zealous pilgrimage to you (think zealously about you and intend to reach you) and keep my drooping (tired) eyelids wide open, looking on darkness as like the blind person see.

Moreover, my soul's imaginary sight present your shadow (image) to my sightless view, which (i.e. your image), like a jewel hung in ghastly night, makes black night beauteous, fresh and new.

See, thus, during the day my body, and during the night my mind for you, and for myself, find no quiet (rest).

Sonnet 28

How can I then return in happy plight,
That am debarr'd the benefit of rest?
When day's oppression is not eased by night,
But day by night, and night by day, oppress'd?

And each, though enemies to either's reign,
Do in consent shake hands to torture me;
The one by toil, the other to complain
How far I toil, still farther off from thee.

I tell the day, to please him, thou art bright,
And dost him grace when clouds do blot the heaven:
So flatter I the swart-complexion'd night;
When sparkling stars twire not, thou gild'st the even.

But day doth daily draw my sorrows longer,
And night doth nightly make grief's strength seem stronger.

Explanation:

How can I return to happy state when I am not allowed the benefit of rest, when Day's oppression (tiredness) is not eased out by Night (i.e. by sleep), but, on the contrary, when the Day becomes more oppressive by (sleepless) Night, and Night becomes more oppressive by (tired – hard worked) Day?

As such, Day and Night are enemies to each other, but they shake hands (become friend) to torture me; one (i.e. the Day) tortures me by toil (making me do hard work) and the other (i.e. the Night) torture me by invoking in my mind the complain that "how far I need to toil, and still I am far off from you".

To please the Day, I tell him that when clouds block the heavenly light, it is only You who grace him by your brightness; and in the same way, I flatter the swart-complexioned (dark) Night saying that when sparkling stars are twire (not visible) that time it is only You who gild the evening.

But still (even after such my flattering and appeasement to Day & to Night) the Day does make daily my sorrow longer, and the Night does make nightly my grief's strength seem stronger!

Sonnet 29

When, in disgrace with fortune and men's eyes,
I all alone beweep my outcast state,
And trouble deaf heaven with my bootless cries,
And look upon myself, and curse my fate,

Wishing me like to one more rich in hope,
Featured like him, like him with friends possess'd,
Desiring this man's art, and that man's scope,
With what I most enjoy contented least;

Yet in these thoughts myself almost despising,
Haply I think on thee, - and then my state
(Like to the lark at break of day arising
From sullen earth) sings hymns at heaven's gate;

For thy sweet love remember'd such wealth brings,
That then I scorn to change my state with kings'.

Explanation:

When, I am in disgrace with my fortune (i.e. lack of good fortune) and with scornful eyes of others, I all alone weep over my outcast (very lower) state, and trouble deaf heaven (heedless God) with my bootless cries (unheard complains & prayers) and look upon myself and curse my bad fate,

Wishing that I be like someone more rich, having skill like him, having large group of loving friends like him, desiring this man's artistic abilities and that man's vast scope, and so much so that I am discontented even with what I used to enjoy the most;

Yet in these thoughts I am almost despising (hating) myself, haply (by chance) I think about you, and then my state (like the lark at break of day arising from the sullen earth) sings hymns (beautiful songs) at heaven's gate;

Because, when your sweet love is remembered, it brings such (inner) wealth (joy) that then I scorn (hate) to exchange my state with the state of Kings!

Sonnet 30

When to the sessions of sweet silent thought
I summon up remembrance of things past,
I sigh the lack of many a thing I sought,
And with old woes new wail my dear time's waste:

Then can I drown an eye, unused to flow,
For precious friends hid in death's dateless night,
And weep afresh love's long-since cancell'd woe,
And moan the expense of many a vanish'd sight.

Then can I grieve at grievances foregone,
And heavily from woe to woe tell o'er
The sad account of fore-bemoaned moan,
Which I new pay as if not paid before.

But if the while I think on thee, dear friend,
All losses are restored, and sorrows end.

Explanation:

When my mind is sweet and silent, and I summon up (recall) remembrance of past things, a sigh arises about the lack of many a thing that I sough, and again sadden my mind with old woes (i.e. memories of past hardships) and that wasted time:

Then my eyes, which are not used to weep, gets wet over the deep sadness of death (death's dateless night) of precious friends, and weep afresh over the past love's longings, and moan (complain) over many a wasted expense:

Then I grieve at past grievances, and grieve even more heavily recalling one woe (one past hardship) after another woe (another past hardship), and pay (suffer) afresh as if not suffered (paid) before, for the sad account of fore-bemoaned (already suffered) moan.

But if the while (if and when) I think on you, dear friend, all (previous) losses are restored, and all sorrows end (such sweet and precious is your love)!

Sonnet 31

Thy bosom is endeared with all hearts,
Which I by lacking have supposed dead;
And there reigns love and all love's loving parts,
And all those friends which I thought buried.

How many a holy and obsequious tear
Hath dear religious love stolen from mine eye,
As interest of the dead, which now appear
But things remov'd, that hidden in thee lie!

Thou art the grave where buried love doth live,
Hung with the trophies of my lovers gone,
Who all their parts of me to thee did give;
That due of many now is thine alone:

Their images I lov'd I view in thee,
And thou (all they) hast all the all of me.

Explanation:

Your bosom (heart) is endeared with all hearts, which I have, by lacking (not being here with me), supposed to be dead; and your heart is the place where rules love and my all loved one's hearts, and all those friends whom I thought to be dead.

Many a holy and obsequious tears (shaded for pleasing others) from my eye have been stolen by dear religious love for paying respect to dead ones; all those dead ones now seem as if living in you.

You are the grave where (that is, you are the one in whose heart) buried love of all my past lovers is alive, and all my past lovers' heart now live in you, and so, my entire love is due for you alone.

Their images that I loved now I view living in you, and you (and all they, as they are now living in you), have all the all of me (that is, you are everyone & everything for me, and I am entirely yours)!

Sonnet 32

If thou survive my well-contented day,
When that churl Death my bones with dust shall cover,
And shalt by fortune once more re-survey
These poor rude lines of thy deceased lover,

Compare them with the bettering of the time;
And though they be outstripp'd by every pen,
Reserve them for my love, not for their rhyme,
Exceeded by the height of happier men.

O, then vouchsafe me but this loving thought:
"Had my friend's Muse grown with this growing age,
A dearer birth than this his love had brought,
To march in ranks of better equipage:

But since he died, and poets better prove,
Theirs for their style I'll read, his for his love."

Explanation:

If you live longer after the end of my well-contended (happy) life, when the death has covered my bones with dust, and if by fortune (by chance) you happen to re-read these poor rude lines (unskilled verses) of your deceased lover (i.e. mine),

And happen to compare them (i.e. my verses) with better lines (verses) written by poets then living, then, preserve my verses (reserve them) for the reason of my love, and don't look at their rhyme (poetic) value, which may be far inferior than (or far exceeded by) the verses of then living happier poets.

O, my love, then vouchsafe me with this loving thought: "Had my friend's Muse grown (advanced) with this present (growing) age, then his love would have given birth to far more dearer verses than this, to march in ranks with the verses of better equipped poets,

But since he died and verses of other poets have proved better in poetic sense than his verses, so, I will read their (other poet's) verses for their better style (for their better poetic quality), but, I will read his (i.e. my friend's) verses for his love".

Sonnet 33

Full many a glorious morning have I seen
Flatter the mountain-tops with sovereign eye,
Kissing with golden face the meadows green,
Gilding pale streams with heavenly alchemy;

Anon permit the basest clouds to ride
With ugly rack on his celestial face,
And from the forlorn world his visage hide,
Stealing unseen to west with this disgrace:

Even so my sun one early morn did shine
With all triumphant splendor on my brow;
But out! alack! he was but one hour mine,
The region cloud hath mask'd him from me now.

Yet him for this my love no whit disdaineth;
Suns of the world may stain, when heaven's sun staineth.

Explanation:

I have seen many a fully glorious mornings when the Sun with his light (sovereign eye) flatter (beautify) mountain-top, kiss the green meadows with its golden face and gild the pale streams with heavenly beauty (with reflected sunlight).

But, soon he (i.e. the Sun) does permit the base clouds to ride with ugly rack (mass of drifting clouds) upon his celestial face and hide his (i.e. Sun's) visage (face) from the forlorn world, and become unseen into west (i.e. set into west) with this disgrace (with this lack of brightness).

In the same way, on one early morning my sun (i.e. my inner light) did shine with all its triumphant splendor on my brow, but out, alack, he (i.e. my inner sun - inner light) was mine only for one hour, then the region cloud (i.e. the cloud of brooding, the cloud of worry, etc) has masked (kept away) him (i.e. my inner light) from me now.

Yet, my love for him (i.e. my love for my inner sun - inner light) do not disdain a whit (do not diminish a bit), as, our inner suns (suns of the world) may stain (become less bright) when the sun of the heaven (i.e. the Celestial Sun) is stained (that is, if the Celestial Sun could stain – could become less bright, our inner suns may also stain).

Sonnet 34

Why didst thou promise such a beauteous day,
And make me travel forth without my cloak,
To let base clouds o'ertake me in my way,
Hiding thy bravery in their rotten smoke?

'Tis not enough that through the cloud thou break,
To dry the rain on my storm-beaten face,
For no man well of such a salve can speak,
That heals the wound, and cures not the disgrace:

Nor can thy shame give physic to my grief;
Though thou repent, yet I have still the loss:
The offender's sorrow lends but weak relief
To him that bears the strong offence's cross,

Ah! but those tears are pearl which thy love sheds,
And they are rich, and ransom all ill deeds.

Explanation:

Why did you promise me such beauteous day and make me travel without my cloak (protecting coat) thereby letting base cloud overtake me in my way, hiding your bravery (cunningness) in their (i.e. clouds') rotten smoke (darkness)?

It is not enough that breaking through the cloud you just dry the rain on my storm-beaten face, as, no man well of than such a slave can say that it would heal my wound and restore the disgrace.

Nor your shame (i.e. being shameful) can give relief to my grief, though you may repent, but still my loss is in tact, as, for one who has suffered a strong offence, the offender's sorrow is but a very weak relief.

Ah! But those tears which you shed (in love for me) are valuable like pearl, and are rich enough to ransom (pay for) all your ill deeds.

Sonnet 35

No more be griev'd at that which thou hast done:
Roses have thorns, and silver fountains mud,
Clouds and eclipses stain both moon and sun,
And loathsome canker lives in sweetest bud.

All men make faults, and even I in this,
Authorizing thy trespass with compare,
Myself corrupting, salving thy amiss,
Excusing thy sins more than thy sins are:

For to thy sensual fault I bring in sense,
(Thy adverse party is thy advocate,)
And 'gainst myself a lawful plea commence:
Such civil war is in my love and hate,

That I an accessary needs must be
To that sweet thief which sourly robs from me.

Explanation:

You need not be much grieved for the fault that you have done: roses have thorns, silver fountains have mud, clouds & eclipses do darken both moon & sun, and loathsome canker (plant disease) lives in sweetest bud (flower).

All human being make faults, and even I am doing the same (i.e. making fault) by authorizing your offence (trespass) with forgiving comparisons (i.e. by offering forgiving allegories), thereby corrupting myself by defending your wrong (amiss), and excusing your sins more than your sins deserve;

Because, to defend your sensual fault (i.e. your unlawful sensual indulgence), I, your adverse party itself being your advocate, bring in cleverness (sense), and against myself commence lawful argument, such civil war is going on in my love and hate,

That I myself, being helper (accessory) in that your sweet theft, must pay by being painfully (sourly) robed (that is, this is such a crime in which I help you in committing robbery against myself, and so, I must pay for it by being painfully robed of your faithfulness towards me, which is my greatest wealth)!

Sonnet 36

Let me confess that we two must be twain,
Although our undivided loves are one:
So shall those blots that do with me remain,
Without thy help, by me be borne alone.

In our two loves there is but one respect,
Though in our lives a separable spite,
Which though it alter not love's sole effect,
Yet doth it steal sweet hours from love's delight.

I may not evermore acknowledge thee,
Lest my bewailed guilt should do thee shame;
Nor thou with public kindness honour me,
Unless thou take that honour from thy name:

But do not so; I love thee in such sort,
As, thou being mine, mine is thy good report.

Explanation:

Let me confess that we two are different (i.e. not one), although our loves are undivided and one, so, let the blots (blemishes) that are upon me remain and borne by me alone, without your help.

In our two loves there is but one respect, though our lives have kept us separated, but which do not alter or make our love's effect less a bit, yet it does steal sweet hours from our love's delight (that is, yet it does reduce our sweet love's delightful time of togetherness).

Now on I shall not acknowledge (that I love) you, lest my bewailed (badly looked upon) guilt shall do shame to you (shall harm your respectfulness), nor shall you honor me with kindness in public, otherwise it will take away honor from your name (spoil your name):

So, don't do so; but I love you in such sort (way) that you being mine, your good report (your good reputation) is mine only!

Sonnet 37

As a decrepit father takes delight
To see his active child do deeds of youth,
So I, made lame by fortune's dearest spite,
Take all my comfort of thy worth and truth;

For whether beauty, birth, or wealth, or wit,
Or any of these all, or all, or more,
Entitled in thy parts do crowned sit,
I make my love engrafted to this store:

So then I am not lame, poor, nor despised,
Whilst that this shadow doth such substance give,
That I in thy abundance am suffic'd
And by a part of all thy glory live.

Look what is best, that best I wish in thee;
This wish I have; then ten times happy me!

Explanation:

As like a decrepit (old & in ill health) father takes delight seeing his active (youthful) child doing excellent deeds worthy of a youth, so do I, who though made lame (disabled) by luck's hard disfavor, do find all my comfort in your worth and truthfulness.

Because, whether beauty, or elite birth, or wealth, or wit (intelligence), or any of these all, or all, or even more, deservedly belongs to you, and upon top of this all your worth, I engraft my love.

So, then, I am not lame, poor, nor despised, as, the fact that I being your part itself, gives me such substance that in your abundance I am sufficed, and I too all your glory live.

Look, whatever that is best, I wish that best in you: and this my wish itself makes me ten times happier!

Sonnet 38

How can my muse want subject to invent,
While thou dost breathe, that pour'st into my verse
Thine own sweet argument, too excellent
For every vulgar paper to rehearse?

O, give thyself the thanks, if aught in me
Worthy perusal stand against thy sight;
For who's so dumb that cannot write to thee,
When thou thyself dost give invention light?

Be thou the tenth muse, ten times more in worth
Than those old nine which rhymers invocate;
And he that calls on thee, let him bring forth
Eternal numbers to outlive long date.

If my slight muse do please these curious days,
The pain be mine, but thine shall be the praise.

Explanation:

How can my Muse want to invent any other subject when you do breathe (i.e. when you are alive) and pour into my verses your own sweet argument, too excellent for all others?

O my love, for all these it is you who is to be thanked. If you find anything worth perusal in me, it is because, who would be so dump that cannot write about you when you yourself do provide such creative inspiration (when you yourself do give invention light)?

You be the tenth Muse, ten times more worthy than those old nine (Nine Muses), which rhymers (poets) invocate (take creative inspiration from); and let him who calls on you (who take creative inspiration from you), bring forth eternal verses (numbers) to live for ever (outlive long date).

If my slight (meager) Muse do create verses pleasing to these curious days (current age), then the pain (trouble) of producing them is mine, but the praise for all that shall be yours!

Sonnet 39

O, how thy worth with manners may I sing,
When thou art all the better part of me?
What can mine own praise to mine own self bring?
And what is 't but mine own, when I praise thee?

Even for this let us divided live,
And our dear love lose name of single one,
That by this separation I may give
That due to thee, which thou deservest alone.

O absence, what a torment wouldst thou prove,
Were it not thy sour leisure gave sweet leave
To entertain the time with thoughts of love,
(Which time and thoughts so sweetly doth deceive,)

And that thou teachest how to make one twain,
By praising him here, who doth hence remain!

Explanation:

O my love, how may I sing (praise) your worth (your beauty, virtues, etc) with manners (i.e. without self-praise), when you are the very core of whatever better that lie in me? What can mine own praise would bring to mine own self? And what is it but mine own (praise) when I praise you? (That is, whatever I say in your praise would amount to be my own self-praise only; such is our oneness with each-other!)

Even for this, let us divided live, and let our dear love lose name of single one, so that, by our this separation, I can give that due (credit, praise) to you which you deserve alone (as, in fact, your virtues, beauty, etc is yours alone, in that there is no contribution of mine).

O my love, what a torment (extreme suffering) your absence would have been proved, if sour (painful) leisure during your absence had not given me sweet leave (sweet opportunity) to entertain the time of your absence with thoughts of love (i.e. with wordless silent visualization about your sweet love), which do transcend (deceive) the time and verbal thoughts (i.e. Wordless silent visualization about your sweet love do transcend the time, and so, my mind).

And thus, your absence teaches me how to make one twain (how to make your Soul live in my wordless silent visualization, and your Physic living away, that way two out of one!) and thereby makes me experience your Soul's presence right here always!

Sonnet 40

Take all my loves, my love, yea, take them all;
What hast thou then more than thou hadst before?
No love, my love, that thou mayst true love call;
All mine was thine, before thou hadst this more.

Then if for my love thou my love receivest,
I cannot blame thee for my love thou usest;
But yet be blam'd, if thou thyself deceivest
By wilful taste of what thyself refusest.

I do forgive thy robbery, gentle thief,
Although thou steal thee all my poverty;
And yet, love knows, it is a greater grief
To bear love's wrong than hate's known injury.

Lascivious grace, in whom all ill well shows,
Kill me with spites: yet we must not be foes.

Explanation:

O my love, take all my love, yea, take them all; what you have more (after adultery) than what you already had? My love, what you call true love is not love; mine everything was yours before you had this more (from someone else).

Then, for the sake of my love if you receive my love, I can not blame you for using my love (for sexual gratification). But, the blame is on you, if you deceive yourself by willfully (intentionally) tasting (enjoying) what you have refused (what you have promised that you will not do - adultery).

O gentle thief, I do forgive your robbery, although you steal from yourself all my poverty (although, you loose my dependence upon your love, you loose my respect for chaste love); and yet, my heart knows, it is a greater grief to bear love's wrong than hate's known injury (that is, my heart knows that it is a greater grief to bear the wrong done by loved one than hard injury inflicted by someone who hates).

O lascivious grace (grace imbued with sexual desire, wanton beauty), in whom all ill appears beautiful, kill me with spites (malice), yet we must not be foes (yet, I will not take you as my enemy).

Sonnet 41

Those petty wrongs that liberty commits
When I am sometime absent from thy heart,
Thy beauty and thy years full well befits,
For still temptation follows where thou art.

Gentle thou art, and therefore to be won,
Beauteous thou art, therefore to be assailed;
And when a woman woos, what woman's son
Will sourly leave her till she have prevailed?

Ah me! but yet thou mightst my seat forbear,
And chide thy beauty and thy straying youth,
Who lead thee in their riot even there
Where thou art forced to break a twofold truth;

Hers, by thy beauty tempting her to thee,
Thine, by thy beauty being false to me.

Explanation:

Those petty wrongs that your liberty (your careless freedom) commits when sometime I am away from you, befits full well to your beauty and youth, as, still temptations (enticing longings of men) follows you wherever you happen to be, or wherever you happen to go.

So gentle you are and therefore you are worthy to be won, so beauteous you are that you shall be assailed (shall be attempted upon to be won in love-making); and when a woman herself woos (try to evoke a man for love-making), will man (woman's son) unpleasantly leave her till she have prevailed (till she has him in love-making)?

But yet, to forbear my seat (to preserve my place in your heart), why you do not chide (rebuke) your beauty and your straying youth, who in its riot (in its spree for sensual gratification) lead you even there where you are forced to break a twofold truth (where you are made so tempted to break following twofold virtue)?

That is, (1) your beauty tempting your youth to break her (your youth's) virtue of remaining chaste, and (2) you losing your virtue of being true (loyal) to me.

Sonnet 42

That thou hast her, it is not all my grief,
And yet it may be said I loved her dearly;
That she hath thee, is of my wailing chief,
A loss in love that touches me more nearly.

Loving offenders, thus I will excuse ye: -
Thou dost love her, because thou know'st I love her;
And for my sake even so doth she abuse me,
Suffering my friend for my sake to approve her.

If I lose thee, my loss is my love's gain,
And, losing her, my friend hath found that loss;
Both find each other, and I lose both twain,
And both for my sake lay on me this cross:

But here's the joy; my friend and I are one;
Sweet flattery! then she loves but me alone.

Explanation:

It is not my grief that you (i.e. Shakespeare's friend) is having her (i.e. Shakespeare's beloved), but my great grief (wailing chief) is the fact that she was mad after you, and she had you (it was not your fault at all), therefore, I forgive you!

You do love her because you know that I love her. It is not less than a suffering for you to approve her in love even after knowing that she abuses me!

I have already lost her, but that my loss has been compensated by your (i.e. my friend's) gain. Now, if I abandon your friendship too, then it would mean her real win, and I will be loosing both of you.

But, for me it is matter of joy that you (i.e. my friend) and I are one (that is, we are still having true & deep friendship), and in that sense, she loves me only (as we both are one), even though this may sound as false self-flattery!

Sonnet 43

When most I wink, then do mine eyes best see,
For all the day they view things unrespected;
But when I sleep, in dreams they look on thee,
And, darkly bright, are bright in dark directed;

Then thou whose shadow shadows doth make bright,
How would thy shadow's form form happy show
To the clear day with thy much clearer light,
When to unseeing eyes thy shade shines so!

How would (I say) mine eyes be blessed made
By looking on thee in the living day,
When in dead night thy fair imperfect shade
Through heavy sleep on sightless eyes doth stay?

All days are nights to see, till I see thee,
And nights, bright days, when dreams do show thee me.

Explanation:

When most I sleep (wink), then my eyes see at its best, as, during the entire day time my eyes keep seeing things that are un-respected (futile), but as I sleep, when in my dreams my eyes look on you, my eyes' (inner) vision become so bright, even in the darkness of night.

If your image (shadow) does make the darkness of night (shadows) so bright, then how much more happy sight (show) your appearance (shadow's form) would produce (form) in the clear day with your so much clearer beauty (light), when even to sleeping (unseeing) eyes your image (shadow) shines so bright!

I say, how much more my eyes would be blessed made by looking on you in the bright (living) day, when in dark (dead) night your fair imperfect image through heavy sleep on sightless (sleeping) eyes does stay?

For me, all days are like nights, till I see you, and all those nights are like bright days, when my dreams do show you to me.

Sonnet 44

If the dull substance of my flesh were thought,
Injurious distance should not stop my way;
For then, despite of space, I would be brought,
From limits far remote, where thou dost stay.

No matter then, although my foot did stand
Upon the farthest earth removed from thee,
For nimble thought can jump both sea and land,
As soon as think the place where he would be.

But ah! thought kills me, that I am not thought,
To leap large lengths of miles when thou art gone,
But that, so much of earth and water wrought,
I must attend time's leisure with my moan;

Receiving nought by elements so slow
But heavy tears, badges of either's woe.

Explanation:

If the dull substance of my body (flesh) were thought, injurious distance should not stop my way, for then, despite of distance (space), I would be brought from far remote distance to the place where you do stay.

Then, it doesn't matter even though I was (my foot did stand) upon the place farthest from you, as, the nimble thought can jump both sea and land, as soon as it think of the place, and it would be there.

But ah! Thought itself kills me that I am not thought and I can not leap large lengths of miles when you are gone, but my body is so much heavy (made up of earth & water) that I must spend (attend) time of our separation (time's leisure) with my moan (with my sadness).

I can not get (receive) anything from this heavy body (which is made up of element so slow, earth & water), except heavy tears, the sign of deep sadness of both of us.

Sonnet 45

The other two, slight air and purging fire,
Are both with thee, wherever I abide;
The first my thought, the other my desire,
These present-absent with swift motion slide.

For when these quicker elements are gone
In tender embassy of love to thee,
My life, being made of four, with two alone
Sinks down to death, oppress'd with melancholy;

Until life's composition be recur'd
By those swift messengers return'd from thee,
Who even but now come back again, assured
Of thy fair health, recounting it to me:

This told, I joy; but then no longer glad,
I send them back again, and straight grow sad.

Explanation:

The other two elements, subtle (slight) air and purging (purifying) fire are both with you, even though wherever I may reside; the first one (air element) is my thought, the other one (fire element) is my desire, and their present & absent occur in swift motion. (Shakespeare wrote about first two elements, earth & water in previous Sonnet No. 44).

As, when these quicker elements (i.e. air & fire – my though & desire) are gone in tender embassy of love to you, my life, which is made up of four elements, is left with merely two (i.e. earth & water) elements alone, sinks down almost to death, oppressed with deep, lasting sadness (melancholy).

Until, the life's composition (natural good structure) is cured again by those swift messengers (i.e. thought & desire) returned from you, who even but now come back again, and assured me of your good (fair) health.

When I am told of this (about your good health), I feel joy, but then, I am no longer glad, as, I send them (i.e. thought & desire) back to you again, and immediately grow sad.

Sonnet 46

Mine eye and heart are at a mortal war
How to divide the conquest of thy sight;
Mine eye my heart thy picture's sight would bar,
My heart mine eye the freedom of that right.

My heart doth plead that thou in him dost lie,
(A closet never pierced with crystal eyes,)
But the defendant doth that plea deny,
And says in him thy fair appearance lies.

To 'cide this title is impanneled
A quest of thoughts, all tenants to the heart;
And by their verdict is determined
The clear eye's moiety, and the dear heart's part:

As thus; mine eye's due is thy outward part,
And my heart's right thy inward love of heart.

Explanation:

My eye and heart are at a mortal war against each-other as to how to share (divide) the treasure (conquest) of your sight; my eye denies (bars) my heart's right of your picture's view, and my heart denies my eye the freedom of that right.

My heart plead (argue) that you in it (i.e. in heart) do live, which is a safest closet never pierced even with crystal eyes. But the defendant (i.e. the defending party – my eye) denies this plea (argument) of the heart, and says that in it (i.e. in eyes) your beautiful appearance resides.

To decide upon this title (i.e. respective rights of both the parties), an inquiry commission (a quest of thoughts) of all tenants of the heart is appointed (impaneled), and by their (i.e. thoughts') verdict the share (moiety) of clear eye and the share (part) of dear heart is determined.

As (per) thus (arrived verdict); my eyes due (legitimate share) is your outward beauty (part), and my heart's right is your inward love of heart (that is, your outward beauty is right of my eyes, and your inward love of heart would be the right of my heart).

Sonnet 47

Betwixt mine eye and heart a league is took,
And each doth good turns now unto the other:
When that mine eye is famish'd for a look,
Or heart in love with sighs himself doth smother,

With my love's picture then my eye doth feast,
And to the painted banquet bids my heart;
Another time mine eye is my heart's guest,
And in his thoughts of love doth share a part:

So, either by thy picture or my love,
Thyself away art present still with me;
For thou not farther than my thoughts canst move,
And I am still with them, and they with thee;

Or if they sleep, thy picture in my sight
Awakes my heart to heart's and eye's delight.

Explanation:

Now, between (betwixt) my eye and my heart a league (alliance) is formed and both of them do help (do good turns) each-other, when my eye is hungry (famished) for your sight, or when my heart is in sigh for your love. (Shakespeare wrote about the war between his eye & his heart in previous Sonnet No. 46).

Then, my eye does feast (cherish) with your (my love's) picture and to that beautiful grand feast (to that painted banquet) invites (bids) my heart too, and at another time, my eye is my heart's guest, and in my heart's happy thoughts of your love do share a part of delight.

So, though you are physically away from me, still either by your picture or by my love (heart) you are present with me, as, you are not farther than my thoughts can reach (move); I am still with my thoughts and my thoughts are with you (that is, you are always present with me, either in my eye as picture, or in my heart as thought).

Or, if my eyes sleep, your image that is in my sight (i.e. in my dream) awakes my heart to my heart's and my eye's delight.

Sonnet 48

How careful was I when I took my way,
Each trifle under truest bars to thrust,
That, to my use, it might unused stay
From hands of falsehood, in sure wards of trust!

But thou, to whom my jewels trifles are,
Most worthy of comfort, now my greatest grief,
Thou, best of dearest, and mine only care,
Art left the prey of every vulgar thief.

Thee have I not lock'd up in any chest,
Save where thou art not, though I feel thou art,
Within the gentle closure of my breast,
From whence at pleasure thou mayst come and part;

And even thence thou wilt be stol'n, I fear,
For truth proves thievish for a prize so dear.

Explanation:

How careful was I when I took my way, my each trifle act was to push you in the safest place of trust (sure ward of trust), where, for my use alone, you stay safe (unused) from the hands of falsehood!

But you, before whom all my jewels are mere trifles, and who is most worthy of comfort, now whose safety is my greatest grief; who is the best of my dearest, and who is the only concern (care) for me, are left unsafe (prey) to be stolen by any common (vulgar) thief.

If not, I have locked you up in a living chest (heart) where you are not physically, though I feel you are, within the gentle closure of my breast, from where you may come and go at pleasure (as and when you wish).

And even from there, I fear, you will be stolen, as, even most truthful person (truth itself) would become thief (prove thievish) for a prize so dear (that is, you are so dear & beautiful that, I fear, even the most truthful person can not prevent himself from becoming a thief).

Sonnet 49

Against that time, if ever that time come,
When I shall see thee frown on my defects,
Whenas thy love hath cast his utmost sum,
  Call'd to that audit by advis'd respects;

Against that time, when thou shalt strangely pass,
And scarcely greet me with that sun, thine eye,
When love, converted from the thing it was,
  Shall reasons find of settled gravity;

Against that time do I ensconce me here
Within the knowledge of mine own desert,
And this my hand against myself uprear,
  To guard the lawful reasons on thy part:

To leave poor me thou hast the strength of laws,
  Since, why to love, I can allege no cause.

Explanation:

In preparation for (against) that time, if ever such time come, when you will see scornfully (frown) towards my defects, when your love had finally evaluated the account of our love-relationship (cast his utmost sum) on the basis of your apparent profit & loss (audit);

In preparation for (against) that time, when you shall strangely walk me by, as if you do not know me, and hardly look at me with your beautiful & bright eye (sun eye), and when your love, diminished from the earlier one, shall try to find serious reasons to end our love-affair;

In preparation for (against) that time, I do take shelter (ensconce me) here, in awareness (knowledge) of my own shortcomings (desert of virtue), and so, this my own hand goes up (up-rear) to give witness against myself, and to guard the lawfulness of your reasons.

So that, you can have good reason (the strength of law) to desert (leave) poor me, since, why you will love me, if I could allege no cause for that (So that, you can have full justification for deserting me, as, if I could not provide you any good reason for loving me, then why you will love me.)

Sonnet 50

How heavy do I journey on the way,
When what I seek - my weary travel's end -
Doth teach that ease and that repose to say,
"Thus far the miles are measured from thy friend!"

The beast that bears me, tired with my woe,
Plods dully on, to bear that weight in me,
As if by some instinct the wretch did know
His rider lov'd not speed, being made from thee:

The bloody spur cannot provoke him on
That sometimes anger thrusts into his hide,
Which heavily he answers with a groan,
More sharp to me than spurring to his side;

For that same groan doth put this in my mind,
My grief lies onward, and my joy behind.

Explanation:

How heavy my journey happens to be on the way when every moment I seek my weary travel's end, and when that ease & repose (brought about by the break in between the journey) brings counting in my mind that "This much miles I have traveled away from my friend!"

The horse (beast) that carries me, tired with my heaviness, walks on slowly & dully to bear that weight in me, as if by some instinct the horse also knew that his rider (i.e. me), who is being made to go away from you, don't want the speed.

The bloody spur can not provoke the horse to walk fast, and sometimes in anger I thrust the spur into his skin, even that also can not make him walk fast, to which he answers heavily with a grown, sharply touching me.

As, that same groan (i.e. horse's groan) does evoke a groan-full sad though in my mind that "My grief lies onwards (as I go ahead in journey), and my joy (i.e. your nearness) is left behind".

Sonnet 51

Thus can my love excuse the slow offence
Of my dull bearer, when from thee I speed:
From where thou art why should I haste me thence?
Till I return, of posting is no need.

O, what excuse will my poor beast then find,
When swift extremity can seem but slow?
Then should I spur, though mounted on the wind;
In winged speed no motion shall I know:

Then can no horse with my desire keep pace;
Therefore desire, of perfect'st love being made,
Shall neigh (no dull flesh) in his fiery race;
But love, for love, thus shall excuse my jade;

Since from thee going he went wilful slow,
Towards thee I'll run, and give him leave to go.

Explanation:

O my love, thus can you please excuse the slow offence (offence of going slow) of my dull horse (bearer) when from you I depart: why should I make haste in departing from the place where you are? There is no need of speeding, till I return back towards you.

O my love, at the time of returning back towards you, what excuse my poor horse will find for running slow, when the speed in its extremity (swift extremity) will seem but slow? Then, though mounted on the wind and going in flying (winged) speed, I shall still feel that I am motionless (standing still) and shall spur (speed up) my horse.

That time, no horse can keep pace with my desire; therefore, in desire of perfect love he (i.e. my horse) shall neigh in his fiery race, so, O my love, for love, please excuse my tired horse.

Since, while departing away from you he went willfully slow, so, while coming back towards you I will run, and will give him leave to go.

Sonnet 52

So am I as the rich, whose blessed key
Can bring him to his sweet up-locked treasure,
The which he will not every hour survey,
For blunting the fine point of seldom pleasure.

Therefore are feasts so solemn and so rare,
Since seldom coming, in the long year set,
Like stones of worth they thinly placed are,
Or captain jewels in the carcanet.

So is the time that keeps you, as my chest,
Or as the wardrobe which the robe doth hide,
To make some special instant special-blest,
By new unfolding his imprison'd pride.

Blessed are you, whose worthiness gives scope,
Being had, to triumph, being lack'd, to hope.

Explanation:

I am like the rich, who by using his blessed key can anytime see his invaluable (sweet) up-locked treasure, but he doesn't see it often, lest the rare pleasure of seeing it might get lessened.

So are the festivals (feasts), so solemn and so rare, since they come seldom over a set time during the year, as like thinly placed precious stones, or as like the Chief (Captain) Jewel in a necklace of jewels (carcanet).

So pride-worthy is the time of your presence, which my heart keeps safe & hidden, as like the wardrobe which keep the special dress (robe) safe and hidden for wearing at some special occasion to make that occasion specially blessed by unfolding afresh the pride-worthy looks.

So blessed you are, and the worthiness of your presence is such that when you are present with me, it is worth triumphant pride, and when you are not present, it is worth hoping for.

Sonnet 53

What is your substance, whereof are you made,
That millions of strange shadows on you tend?
Since every one hath, every one, one's shade,
And you, but one, can every shadow lend.

Describe Adonis, and the counterfeit
Is poorly imitated after you:
On Helen's cheek all art of beauty set,
And you in Grecian tires are painted new:

Speak of the spring, and foison of the year;
The one doth shadow of your beauty show,
The other as your bounty doth appear,
And you in every blessed shape we know.

In all external grace you have some part,
But you like none, none you, for constant heart.

Explanation:

What is the substance whereof you are made, that millions of strange images appear fitting in you? Since, every one has only one shade (look), but you are the only one who can encompass all other shadows (looks).

Take Adonis (In Greek Mythology, very handsome young man loved by Aphrodite), his picture poorly resembles your beauty; and all the art of beauty that is there on Helen's cheeks is painted anew in you in ancient Greece style.

Take the spring and harvest (foison) seasons of the year: in spring the shadow of your beauty appears, and in harvest the bountifulness of your heart does appear, but you appear in every blessed shape that we know.

In all external beauty (grace) you have some part, but no one has the constant (loyal & ever love emanating) heart like the one you have.

Sonnet 54

O, how much more doth beauty beauteous seem
By that sweet ornament which truth doth give!
The rose looks fair, but fairer we it deem
For that sweet odour which doth in it live.

The canker-blooms have full as deep a dye
As the perfumed tincture of the roses,
Hang on such thorns, and play as wantonly
When summer's breath their masked buds discloses:

But, for their virtue only is their show,
They live unwoo'd, and unrespected fade;
Die to themselves. Sweet roses do not so;
Of their sweet deaths are sweetest odours made:

And so of you, beauteous and lovely youth,
When that shall fade, my verse distills your truth.

Explanation:

How much more beauty does beauteous (more beautiful) seem by that sweet ornament which truth does give! Rose is beautiful but we take (deem) it as even more beautiful because of the sweet smell that dwells in it.

The canker blooms (dog roses, which are red but scentless) has full and deep color like the perfumed color (tincture) of the roses, and like roses they hang on such thorns, and play as wantonly (in luxurious pleasure) when summer's wind (breath) blooms their masked buds.

But, since, their virtue is only in their show (since, they are beautiful merely in looks) they live unloved (unwoo'd,) and un-respected fade, and die to themselves. But that is not the case with sweet roses, as, on their sweet death the sweetest scent is made from it.

And so is the case of you, when your beauteous and lovely youth shall fade (age), my verse (poem) shall keep alive (distill) your truth, beauty & youth.

Sonnet 55

Not marble, nor the gilded monuments
Of princes, shall outlive this powerful rhyme;
But you shall shine more bright in these contents
Than unswept stone, besmear'd with sluttish time.

When wasteful war shall statues overturn,
And broils root out the work of masonry,
Nor Mars his sword nor war's quick fire shall burn
The living record of your memory.

'Gainst death and all-oblivious enmity
Shall you pace forth; your praise shall still find room,
Even in the eyes of all posterity
That wear this world out to the ending doom.

So, till the judgment that yourself arise,
You live in this, and dwell in lovers' eyes.

Explanation:

Not marble, nor the gilded monuments of princes shall outlive this powerful poem (rhyme); you will shine more bright in the content of these lines than un-cleaned (un-swept) monuments (stone) damaged (besmeared) by the long passage of time (sluttish time).

When wasteful war shall destroy (overturn) status (of all renowned people), and when broils (violence) shall root out all work of sculpting & building (masonry), no sword of Mars nor quick fire of war shall destroy living record of your memory contained in this my poem.

Against death and injurious oblivion you shall live (pace forth); your praise (contained in this poem) shall still find the place (room) even in the eyes of all generations to come (posterity), and shall outlast this world till the ending doom.

So, till the judgment day when you arise from the dead, you shall live in this (poem), and you shall dwell in lovers' eyes.

Sonnet 56

Sweet love, renew thy force; be it not said,
Thy edge should blunter be than appetite,
Which but to-day by feeding is allay'd,
To-morrow sharpen'd in his former might:

So, love, be thou; although to-day thou fill
Thy hungry eyes, even till they wink with fullness,
To-morrow see again, and do not kill
The spirit of love with a perpetual dullness.

Let this sad interim like the ocean be
Which parts the shore, where two contracted-new
Come daily to the banks, that, when they see
Return of love, more blest may be the view;

Or call it winter, which, being full of care,
Makes summer's welcome thrice more wish'd, more rare.

Explanation:

O sweet love, renew thy force; let not your edge (intensity) be blunt (less sharp) than appetite, which is satisfied (allayed) to-day by feeding, but to-morrow sharpened again with former intensity (might).

So, my love, be yourself; to-day you satisfy your hungry eyes (by beholding beloved) till they wink (close) with fullness, in the same way to-morrow also you behold the beloved, but do not kill the spirit of love with a lasting dullness (that is, keep your eyes' hunger for beholding beloved daily new).

Let this sad interval (period of absence) be like the ocean, which parts (separates) the shore, where two (lovers) come daily, and when they see each-other returned (return of love), they feel the view (of beholding each-other afresh again) even more blessed.

Or else call it (the period of absence, sad interim) winter, which because needing much more care, makes summer's welcome thrice more wished, and more rare. (In England summer is short and very pleasant warm season).

Sonnet 57

Being your slave, what should I do but tend
Upon the hours and times of your desire?
I have no precious time at all to spend,
Nor services to do, till you require.

Nor dare I chide the world-without-end hour,
Whilst I, my sovereign, watch the clock for you,
Nor think the bitterness of absence sour,
When you have bid your servant once adieu;

Nor dare I question with my jealous thought
Where you may be, or your affairs suppose,
But, like a sad slave, stay and think of nought,
Save, where you are how happy you make those:

So true a fool is love, that in your will
(Though you do any thing) he thinks no ill.

Explanation:

Being your slave, what would I do except to wait for the hour & time when you desire to be with me? My time is not precious at all; I have no important works to do, except to serve you (that is, my time is not precious at all till you require it).

O my sovereign, neither I dare to chide (curse) very slow moving, as if never ending (world-without-end) hour, while I wait (watch the clock) for your return, nor I think your absence bitter when you are gone biding me (i.e. your servant) goodbye.

Neither dare I to jealously question your whereabouts, nor I suppose your affair with others, but, like a sad slave, I stay and think nothing except, how happy you make those where you are (that is, how happy you make those with whom you are spending time).

Truly so fool is love that in wish of having you, he thinks nothing ill (bad), even though you may do anything (That is, truly love is so fool that in wish of getting you, he thinks nothing bad about you, even though you do anything).

Sonnet 58

That god forbid, that made me first your slave,
I should in thought control your times of pleasure,
Or at your hand the account of hours to crave,
Being your vassal, bound to stay your leisure!

O, let me suffer (being at your beck)
The imprison'd absence of your liberty,
And patience, tame to sufferance, bide each check
Without accusing you of injury.

Be where you list; your charter is so strong,
That you yourself may privilege your time:
Do what you will, to you it doth belong
Yourself to pardon of self-doing crime.

I am to wait, though waiting so be hell;
Not blame your pleasure, be it ill or well.

Explanation:

That God, who made me your slave, forbid me from thinking about controlling your time of pleasure, or asking the account of your time (as to how & where you spent it). I, being your vassal (loyal slave), am bound to stay at your leisure (bound to stay waiting for you, till you come at your wish)!

O, I am being at your beck & call, let me suffer imprisoned absence of your liberty; and let me tame my patience to endure each restrain that you may impose, without accusing you of injury.

Be wherever you wish, your power (charter) is so strong that it is your own privilege to spend your time as you wish; and it is well within your power to pardon yourself for all your self-done crime.

I will wait, though so waiting is like hell, and will never blame your pleasure (enjoyment), be it good or bad.

Sonnet 59

If there be nothing new, but that which is
Hath been before, how are our brains beguil'd,
Which labouring for invention bear amiss
The second burthen of a former child!

O, that record could with a backward look,
Even of five hundred courses of the sun,
Show me your image in some antique book,
Since mind at first in character was done!

That I might see what the old world could say
To this composed wonder of your frame;
Whether we are mended, or whether better they,
Or whether revolution be the same.

O, sure I am, the wits of former days
To subjects worse have given admiring praise.

Explanation:

If there is nothing new and that everything which is (now) has been before, then how our minds are deceived (beguiled), which labor for inventing that thing which is already there, like bearing the pregnancy pain second time for a same former child!

I wonder, could the past record, on look back of even five hundred years (five hundred courses of the sun), show me your image (show me beauty like you) in some antique book, since the time human mind was first expressed into writings (since mind at first in character was done)!

So that I might see (assume) what the old generation (old world) could say about this your so wonderfully composed picture (frame), whether we are better or whether they were better or whether both generations are the same (or whether revolution be the same).

But, I am sure that the wits of former days (minds of former generation writers) have given admiring praise to worse subjects (that is, I am sure that former writers have given admiring praise to subjects less beautiful and less admirable than you – I am sure, no one as beautiful and as admirable as you has ever walked on this earth before)!

Sonnet 60

Like as the waves make towards the pebbled shore,
So do our minutes hasten to their end;
Each changing place with that which goes before.
In sequent toil all forwards do contend.

Nativity, once in the main of light,
Crawls to maturity, wherewith being crown'd,
Crooked eclipses 'gainst his glory fight,
And Time, that gave, doth now his gift confound.

Time doth transfix the flourish set on youth,
And delves the parallels in beauty's brow;
Feeds on the rarities of nature's truth,
And nothing stands but for his scythe to mow.

And yet, to times in hope, my verse shall stand,
Praising thy worth, despite his cruel hand.

Explanation:

Like as the waves proceed towards the pebbled (smoothened) shore, so do our minutes (time) move fast (hasten) to their end; each moment taking place of the former one (that which gone before), thus all toiling, one after another (in sequent toil) to move forward.

The childhood (nativity), which was once in lime light, slowly becomes mature (crawls to maturity) and flourishes most (wherewith being crowned), but then crooked eclipses (the passage of time) reduces its glory, and that very Time which has given the youth everything, itself now destroys what it has given.

Time does paralyze the glory (transfix the flourish) that is set on the youth, and inscribes wrinkles on beautiful brow (delves the parallels in beauty's brow), by eating therefrom the cuteness & youthfulness that nature has bestowed (feeds on the rarities of nature's truth), and nothing can stand against the mowing of time's scythe (that is, everything is destroyed by scythe of time).

And yet, my verse (poem) shall, praising your worth (praising your beauty & virtues), stand still for ever, against time's cruel, all destroying hand.

Sonnet 61

Is it thy will thy image should keep open
My heavy eyelids to the weary night?
Dost thou desire my slumbers should be broken,
While shadows, like to thee, do mock my sight?

Is it thy spirit that thou send'st from thee
So far from home, into my deeds to pry;
To find out shames and idle hours in me,
The scope and tenure of thy jealousy?

O no! Thy love, though much, is not so great;
It is my love that keeps mine eye awake;
Mine own true love that doth my rest defeat,
To play the watchman ever for thy sake:

For thee watch I, whilst thou dost wake elsewhere,
From me far off, with others all-too-near.

Explanation:

Is it your will your image that keeps my heavy eyelids (heavy with sleepiness) open in this weary (tired) night? Do you desire that my sleep (slumber) be broken, while images (shadows), like to you, do mock my sight (that is, do you wish that your images move here & there in my inner sight, and destroy my sleep)?

Is it your spirit that you sent from you, so far from home, to spy (pry) my deeds to find out something shameful (disloyal) in my deeds during those hours when you are away from me, in the scope and tenure of your jealousy?

O no, though your love for me is much, but it is not so great: it is my love for you that keeps my eye awake, my own true love is such that it keeps me ever watchful (play the watchman) for your sake, and does defeat my sleep (rest).

For, I watch you (I watch your image in my inner sight) when you are awake elsewhere, very far away from me, but all-too-near with others (in all-too-near company of others).

Sonnet 62

Sin of self-love possesseth all mine eye,
And all my soul, and all my every part;
And for this sin there is no remedy,
It is so grounded inward in my heart.

Methinks no face so gracious is as mine,
No shape so true, no truth of such account,
And for myself mine own worth do define,
As I all other in all worths surmount.

But when my glass shows me myself indeed,
Beated and chopp'd with tann'd antiquity,
Mine own self-love quite contrary I read,
Self so self-loving were iniquity,

'Tis thee (myself) that for my self I praise,
Painting my age with beauty of thy days.

Explanation:

Sin of self-love possesses all mine eye, all my soul and all my every part, and for this my sin there is no remedy, as this self-love is so deeply embedded (grounded inward) in my heart.

Methinks no other face as gracious as mine, no other beauty comparable to mine (no shape so true as mine), no one as virtuous as me (no truth of such account), and my own worth is defined by myself only, as, I surpass (surmount) all others in every way (in all worths).

But when my mirror (glass) indeed shows me myself (my physical self), overpowered (beated) and wrinkle-skinned by aging (with tanned antiquity), I read (see) my own self-love quite contrary, and think that the self, so self-loving is unfair (iniquity).

O my love, it is you, who reside in each & every part of mine, as my inner self, and for that I praise myself, by painting myself with the beauty of your worth.

Sonnet 63

Against my love shall be, as I am now,
With Time's injurious hand crush'd and o'erworn;
When hours have drain'd his blood, and fill'd his brow
With lines and wrinkles; when his youthful morn

Hath travell'd on to age's Steepy night;
And all those beauties, whereof now he's king,
Are vanishing or vanish'd out of sight,
Stealing away the treasure of his spring;

For such a time do I now fortify
Against confounding age's cruel knife,
That he shall never cut from memory
My sweet love's beauty, though my lover's life.

His beauty shall in these black lines be seen,
And they shall live, and he in them, still green.

Explanation:

In preparation for the time when the Time's injurious hand has, as I am now, crushed and over worn my beloved, and when hours (Time) has drained my love's blood, and filled my love's forehead with lines and wrinkles;

When my love's youth has traveled on and has aged, and when all those beauties of which now my love is king are vanishing or vanished out of sight, stealing away the treasure of my love's spring (youthfulness).

For such a time, now, by writing this poem, I do fortify (do prepare) against the destroying age's (Time's) cruel knife, so that the Time shall never be able to cut from memory my sweet love's beauty, even after my lover's life (death).

My love's beauty shall always be seen in these black lines (in this poem), and this poem, and in it my beloved, shall live ever green.

Sonnet 64

When I have seen by time's fell hand defac'd
The rich-proud cost of outworn buried age;
When some lofty towers I see down-razed,
And brass eternal, slave to mortal rage;

When I have seen the hungry ocean gain
Advantage on the kingdom of the shore,
And the firm soil win of the watery main
Increasing store with loss, and loss with store;

When I have seen such interchange of state,
Or state itself confounded to decay;
Ruin hath taught me thus to ruminate -
That time will come and take my love away.

This thought is a death, which cannot choose
But weep to have, that which it fears to lose.

Explanation:

When I have seen the ruins of rich and proud buried age by the cruel (fell) course of the times; when I see some lofty towers destroyed (down-raged), and when I see that the eternal seeming brass is also slave to mortal rage (subject to destruction).

When I have seen (during the time of tide) the hungry ocean gain advantage on the kingdom of the shore, and the firm soil resist the strength of tide, and thus, both trying to increase their respective expand (store) at the loss of the other.

When I have seen such interchange of state (one's loss, other's gain), or seen that that state itself is doomed to decay; this ruin has taught me to ruminate (contemplate – meditate) thus that "time will come and will take away my love from me".

This thought (of losing you) itself is like a death for me, and I have no choice but to weep to have your love, which I fear to lose.

Sonnet 65

Since brass, nor stone, nor earth, nor boundless sea,
But sad mortality o'er sways their power,
How with this rage shall beauty hold a plea,
Whose action is no stronger than a flower?

O, how shall summer's honey breath hold out
Against the wrackful siege of battering days,
When rocks impregnable are not so stout,
Nor gates of steel so strong, but time decays?

O fearful meditation! Where, alack!
Shall Time's best jewel from Time's chest lie hid?
Or what strong hand can hold his swift foot back?
Or who his spoil to beauty can forbid?

O none, unless this miracle have might,
That in black ink my love shall still shine bright.

Explanation:

Since the sad mortality destroys (over sways) the power of brass, stone, earth and boundless sea, then against this rage (destruction), how beauty, whose action is not stronger that a flower, shall save itself?

O, how shall the honey (beauty) of summer survive (breath hold out) against the painful attack (wreckful siege) of destroying Time (battering days), when the strongest rocks are not so stout, nor gates of steel so strong to withstand the decay of Time?

O my sad & fearful contemplation, shall my love's beauty (Time's best jewel) remain hidden (unaffected) from Time's purview, or what strong hand can hold back Time's swift foot, or who can forbid the spoilage of beauty by Time?

O, none, unless this miracle (i.e. this poem) has such might that in its lines (in black ink), my love shall still shine bright, for ever.

Sonnet 66

Tir'd with all these, for restful death I cry,-
As, to behold desert a beggar born,
And needy nothing trimm'd in jollity,
And purest faith unhappily forsworn,

And gilded honour shamefully misplac'd,
And maiden virtue rudely strumpeted,
And right perfection wrongfully disgrac'd,
And strength by limping sway disabled,

And art made tongue-tied by authority,
And folly (doctor-like) controlling skill,
And simple truth miscall'd simplicity,
And captive good attending captain ill:

Tir'd with all these, from these would I be gone,
Save that, to die, I leave my love alone.

Explanation:

Tired with all these (following), I cry for restful death - as, to behold desert I born as beggar, and I am needy having no jollity (state of joy), and purest faith is unhappily forsworn.

And gilded honor is bestowed upon undeserved (shamefully misplaced), and virtue of virginity is rudely condemned, and right perfection is wrongfully disgraced, and strength is disabled by limping sway (influence).

And the art is made tongue-tied by authority (power), and folly (as if it knows all) is controlling skill, and simple truth is taken as idiocy, and the good is a prisoner (captive) in the hands of evil.

Tired with all these, I would have already gone from this world, but to die would mean leaving my love (i.e. you) alone.

Sonnet 67

Ah, wherefore with infection should he live,
And with his presence grace impiety,
That sin by him advantage should achieve,
And lace itself with his society?

Why should false painting imitate his cheek,
And steal dead seeing of his living hue?
Why should poor beauty indirectly seek
Roses of shadow, since his rose is true?

Why should he live now Nature bankrupt is,
Beggar'd of blood to blush through lively veins?
For she has no exchequer now but his,
And, proud of many, lives upon his gains.

O, him she stores, to show what wealth she had
In day long since, before these last so bad.

Explanation:

Ah, for what reason (wherefore) he should live in the age of corruption (with infection), and his presence (existence) grace the impiety (impurity), and by that, why that sin (impiety) get advantage of establishing itself with his society?

Why should false painting imitate his cheek and convert his living beauty into a dead painting (seeing)? Why should poor beauty indirectly (by imitation) seek painted roses (roses of shadow), when his rose is true?

Why should he live when the Nature is bankrupt and beggared (robbed) of blood to blush (glow) through lively veins? For, the nature has no exchequer (treasure) except him, and, proud of many, she lives upon his gains (accumulations).

O, she stores him to show what wealth she had in those past days (when he was), before these present (last) bad days.

Sonnet 68

Thus is his cheek the map of days outworn,
When beauty lived and died as flowers do now,
Before these bastard signs of fair were born,
Or durst inhabit of a living brow;

Before the golden tresses of the dead,
The right of sepulchres were shorn away,
To live a second life on second head,
Ere beauty's dead fleece made another gay:

In him those holy antique hours are seen,
Without all ornament, itself, and true,
Making no summer of another's green,
Robbing no old to dress his beauty new;

And him as for a map doth Nature store,
To show false Art what beauty was of yore.

Explanation:

This is his cheek, the map (pattern) of the worn out (past) days, when the beauty truly lived and died as do flowers now, before these false (bastard) signs of beauty (fair) were born or inhibited on a living brow (that is, before people started wearing these artificial beauty make-ups on their faces).

Before beautiful hairs (golden tresses) of the dead, which should have been buried into sepulcher (grave), were cut (shorn) away to make them into a wig, to make them live a second life on a second head (to be worn by another person).

In him those pure beauty-treasure of antique time (holy antique hours) is seen, without any ornament, itself, and true, without making himself more youthful (summer) from borrowed (another's) green, and without robbing old (without wearing wig etc) to dress his beauty new.

And the Nature does store (preserve) him as for a map (as for an example), to show to false Art (current make-up art) what was the beauty of yore (that is, the Nature does store him for an example to show to the current time what was the beauty of the past antique time).

Sonnet 69

Those parts of thee that the world's eye doth view
Want nothing that the thought of hearts can mend:
All tongues (the voice of souls) give thee that due,
Uttering bare truth, even so as foes commend.

Thine outward thus with outward praise is crowned;
But those same tongues that give thee so thine own,
In other accents do this praise confound,
By seeing farther than the eye hath shown.

They look into the beauty of thy mind,
And that, in guess, they measure by thy deeds;
Then (churls) their thoughts, although their eyes were kind,
To thy fair flower add the rank smell of weeds:

But why, thy odour matcheth not thy show,
The solve is this, - that thou dost common grow.

Explanation:

Those your (outer beautiful) parts that are visible to people's eye (the world's eye) are perfect, and nothing is lacking in that which heart wish to mend; all tongues (the voice of souls), both of friends and foes, uttering bare truth (truth only) in praise give you what is truly due.

Your outward beauty is crowned by outward praises, but those same tongues that give you so much praise, when they look deeper than your outward beauty, right into your heart, do utter other accent and nullify (confound) this praise;

They look into your heart for inner beauty (the beauty of your mind), and that, in guess, they measure by your deeds, then, (not finding your deeds as beautiful as your looks) they think ill of you (churl their thoughts), although they still appreciate your outward beauty (although their eyes were kind).

But why, the fragrance of your deeds is not matching with your beautiful looks (show), the answer for this is that - you yourself look within and grow your inner beauty as well.

Sonnet 70

That thou art blamed shall not be thy defect,
For slander's mark was ever yet the fair;
The ornament of beauty is suspect,
A crow that flies in heaven's sweetest air,

So thou be good, slander doth but approve
Thy worth the greater, being woo'd of time;
For canker vice the sweetest buds doth love,
And thou present'st a pure unstained prime.

Thou hast pass'd by the ambush of young days,
Either not assailed, or victor being charged;
Yet this thy praise cannot be so thy praise,
To tie up envy, evermore enlarged:

If some suspect of ill mask'd not thy show,
Then thou alone kingdoms of hearts should'st owe.

Explanation:

The fact that you are blamed shall not be your fault, as, that which is fair (unblemished) is always the target (mark) of slender (accusation); the ornament of beauty is suspect, like a crow that flies in heave's sweetest air.

So you be good, the slander (accusation) only proves that your worth is even greater, and would be cherished for times to come (being wooed of time), because, the canker vice (disease) love to attack sweetest buds, whereas, your youth (prime) is pure & unstained.

You have passed by the ambush (lures) of young days, either not assailed (not attacked), or you have won those attacks (lures), yet this your praise cannot be enough to control (tie up) evermore enlarged envy of others.

If some suspects of ill (such slanders) have not masked your beauty (show), then you alone would have won the kingdoms of hearts (that is, if such suspects have not masked your beauty, then you alone would have won the hearts of all).

Sonnet 71

No longer mourn for me when I am dead
Than you shall hear the surly sullen bell
Give warning to the world that I am fled
From this vile world, with vilest worms to dwell;

Nay, if you read this line, remember not
The hand that writ it; for I love you so,
That I in your sweet thoughts would be forgot,
If thinking on me then should make you woe.

O, if (I say) you look upon this verse,
When I perhaps compounded am with clay,
Do not so much as my poor name rehearse;
But let your love even with my life decay:

Lest the wise world should look into your moan,
And mock you with me after I am gone.

Explanation:

When I am dead, no longer mourn for me than the time you hear funeral church bell (surly sullen bell), declaring to the world that I am dead from this vile world, to dwell in grave with vilest worms.

If you read this line (poem), don't remember the hand that wrote it, because, I love you so much that, I would prefer to be forgotten than you become sad by thinking on me.

O, I say, if you look upon this poem when I am buried, and perhaps became the clay, do not utter (rehearse) my poor name, but let your love for me die with my death.

Otherwise, the wise (cleaver) world would look into your moan, and mock (deride) you for thinking about me after I am gone (dead).

Sonnet 72

O, lest the world should task you to recite,
What merit lived in me, that you should love
After my death, - dear love, forget me quite,
For you in me can nothing worthy prove;

Unless you would devise some virtuous lie,
To do more for me than mine own desert,
And hang more praise upon deceased I
Than niggard truth would willingly impart:

O, lest your true love may seem false in this,
That you for love speak well of me untrue,
My name be buried where my body is,
And live no more to shame nor me not you.

For I am shamed by that which I bring forth,
And so should you, to love things nothing worth.

Explanation:

O, dear love, lest the world tax (task) you to count (recite) what merit were in me that you should love me after my death, so, dear love, forget me quite, for you can not prove anything worthy in me.

Unless you would devise some virtuous lie to do more for me than my worthlessness (mine own desert), and bestow (hang) more praise upon deceased me than niggard truth would rightly reveal (impart).

O, lest your true love may seem false in this, that for love's sake you speak untrue in praise (well) of me, so, let my name be buried in grave with my body, and live no more to shame nor me nor you.

For I am shamed by my real worth (by that which I bring forth), and so should you, to love some one (like me) of no worth.

Sonnet 73

That time of year thou mayest in me behold
When yellow leaves, or none, or few, do hang
Upon those boughs which shake against the cold,
Bare ruined choirs, where late the sweet birds sang,

In me thou seest the twilight of such day
As after sunset fadeth in the west,
Which by and by black night doth take away,
Death's second self, that seals up all in rest.

In me thou seest the glowing of such fire,
That on the ashes of his youth doth lie,
As the death-bed whereon it must expire,
Consumed with that which it was nourished by,

This thou perceiv'st which makes thy love more strong,
To love that well which thou must leave ere long.

Explanation:

You would behold (notice) in me that time of year (i.e. autumn), when yellow leaves, or no leaves, or few leaves, do hang upon those boughs (branches) which shake against cold wind (of winter) like bare ruined choirs, where once sweet birds used to sing.

You would see in me the twilight of such day, as after sunset fade in the west, and which, by and by, is taken away by black nights, the death's second self, that encompasses (seals up) all in the rest (in the sleep).

You would see in me the glowing of such fire, that lies on the ashes of my youth, as the death bed whereon that glow must expire, consumed with that (i.e. life) by which it was nourished.

When you will perceive all this in me, it would make your love more strong, and would make you love that (i.e. me) even more (well), which you must leave ere long (in short time).

Sonnet 74

But be contented: when that fell arrest
Without all bail shall carry me away,
My life hath in this line some interest,
Which for memorial still with thee shall stay.

When thou reviewest this, thou dost review
The very part was consecrate to thee.
The earth can have but earth, which is his due;
My spirit is thine, the better part of me:

So then thou hast but lost the dregs of life,
The prey of worms, my body being dead;
The coward conquest of a wretch's knife,
Too base of thee to be remembered.

The worth of that, is that which it contains,
And that is this, and this with thee remains.

Explanation:

But be contended (assured), when that (i.e. death) arrest me without any bail and carry me away, my life shall still live as memorial in this line (poem), and shall stay (remain) with you.

When you look back upon (review) this poem, you would see (review) the very part which was devoted (consecrate) to you; the earth can have only my body, which is earth's due, but my spirit, the better part of me, is yours alone.

So, then (i.e. upon my death) you would have lost only my body, the dregs of life, the prey (food) of worms, the coward conquest of a wretch's knife, and being dead, it would be too base to be remembered.

The worth of that (i.e. body), is that which (i.e. spirit) it contains, and that (i.e. my spirit) is this (i.e. expression of my love in this poem), and which (i.e. my love, my spirit) will remain with you.

Sonnet 75

So are you to my thoughts, as food to life,
Or as sweet-season'd showers are to the ground,
And for the peace of you I hold such strife,
As `twixt a miser and his wealth is found:

Now proud as an enjoyer, and anon
Doubting the filching age will steal his treasure;
Now counting best to be with you alone,
Then better'd that the world may see my pleasure:

Sometime all full with feasting on thy sight,
And by and by clean starved for a look;
Possessing or pursuing no delight,
Save what is had or must from you be took.

Thus do I pine and surfeit day by day,
Or gluttoning on all, or all away.

Explanation:

So are you to my thoughts, as food to life, or as right-timed rains (sweet-seasoned showers) are to the land; and for the sake of peace of you, I take on such strife (fight), as does the miser for his wealth.

Now proud as an enjoyer, and soon (anon) doubting that the filching age (thief Time) will steal this treasure (i.e. you); now thinking that it is best to be with you alone, and soon feel prouder in letting world see my pleasure (of being with you).

Sometime fully satisfied (all full) with feasting (enjoying) on your sight (by love-fully beholding you), and by and by wholly starved for your look, possessing or pursuing no other delight than what I have or will have (receive) from you.

Thus, sometime I do pine (starve), and sometime I do enjoy abundance (surfeit), in other words, either devouring (gluttoning) the whole, or completely starved (all away).

Sonnet 76

Why is my verse so barren of new pride?
So far from variation or quick change?
Why, with the time, do I not glance aside
To new-found methods and to compounds strange?

Why write I still all one, ever the same,
And keep invention in a noted weed,
That every word doth almost tell my name
Showing their birth, and where they did proceed?

O, know, sweet love, I always write of you,
And you and love are still my argument;
So all my best is dressing old words new,
Spending again what is already spent;

For as the sun is daily new and old,
So is my love still telling what is told.

Explanation:

Why is my verse (poem) so barren of new style (pride)? Why is my verse so far from variation or quick change? Why do I not glance aside to use new-found methods and to use compounds new, as the time change?

Why still I write all one, ever the same, and rarely use new invention, and why every word that I use almost bears my signature, showing from where they sprang, and where they proceed?

O my sweet love, know that I always write about you; you and love are still the subjects of my poems, so all my best is to use the same words about you in new ways, describing (spending) again what is already described (spent).

For as the sun is daily new and old, so is my love, still (always) telling what is already told.

Sonnet 77

Thy glass will show thee how thy beauties wear,
Thy dial how thy precious minutes waste;
The vacant leaves thy mind's imprint will bear,
And of this book, this learning mayst thou taste.

The wrinkles which thy glass will truly show,
Of mouthed graves will give thee memory;
Thou by thy dial's shady stealth may'st know
Time's thievish progress to eternity.

Look what thy memory cannot contain,
Commit to these waste blacks, and thou shalt find
These children nursed, deliver'd from thy brain,
To take a new acquaintance of thy mind.

These offices, so oft as thou wilt look,
Shall profit thee, and much enrich thy book.

Explanation:

Your mirror (glass) will show you how profound your beauty was, and your clock (dial) will show you how your precious time was passed (minutes waste); the blank pages (vacant leaves) will be printed (filled) by your memory (mind's imprint), and you will enjoy the reading of this book.

The wrinkles, the mouthed graves on your face, which your glass will truly show, will give you the memory; and by your clock's quiet & secret move (dial's shady stealth) you shall know time's thieving (stealing) passage towards eternity.

Look, what your memory is not clear, leave (commit) it to these blank pages, and you shall find that, over a time, these blank pages shall, like your well nursed brain children, be filled by refreshed memory (new acquaintance) of your mind.

So often as you will look upon these pages of your memory book (these offices), it will profit you, and will much enrich your book (will make your book of memory more full & rich).

Sonnet 78

So oft have I invoked thee for my muse,
And found such fair assistance in my verse,
As every alien pen hath got my use,
And under thee their poesy disperse.

Thine eyes, that taught the dumb on high to sing,
And heavy ignorance aloft to fly,
Have added feathers to the learned's wing,
And given grace a double majesty.

Yet be most proud of that which I compile,
whose influence is thine, and born of thee:
In others' works thou does but mend the style,
And arts with thy sweet graces graced be;

But thou art all my art, and dost advance
As high as learning my rude ignorance.

Explanation:

So often I have invoked you for my muse (for formulating poetry-thought in my mind), and every time I have found its fair assistance in my verse (poem). All other poets (every alien pen) are using this same my technique, and thus under your influence their poetry flourish (poesy disperse).

Your eyes have taught even the dumb on high to sing, and have added feathers to the learned's wing, to make heavy ignorance an aloft flying wisdom, and have given double majesty to grace (has made the grace a doubly majestic).

Yet be most profound (proud) in that which I compile (in my poems), of which you are the only influence, and which is born of you. In others' works (poems) you do but only improve (mend) their style, and with your sweet grace their arts do become more graceful.

But for me you are all my art, and you make my art so advance that even my rude ignorance turns into learning (that is, you make my art so advance that even my basest ignorance turns into ever expanding & increasing wisdom).

Sonnet 79

Whilst I alone did call upon thy aid,
My verse alone had all thy gentle grace;
But now my gracious numbers are decay'd,
And my sick muse doth give another place.

I grant, sweet love, thy lovely argument
Deserves the travail of a worthier pen;
Yet what of thee thy poet doth invent,
He robs thee of, and pays it thee again.

He lends thee virtue, and he stole that word
From thy behaviour; beauty doth he give,
And found it in thy cheek; he can afford
No praise to thee but what in thee doth live.

Then thank him not for that which he doth say,
Since what he owes thee thou thy self doth pay.

Explanation:

When I alone did call upon your aid (help), my verse alone had all your gentle grace, but now my gracious poems (numbers) has decayed, and my sick muse (weak creative faculty) does concede its place to another.

Sweet love, I grant that lovely subject (argument) of your beauty deserve the labor (travail) of a more worthy poet (of a worthier pen); yet what your poet invent of you, is like robbing from you, and paying it to you again.

He (poet) lends virtue to you, but he stole that word (word about your virtue) from your behaviour only; whatever he write of the beauty, it is found in your cheek: he can afford (provide) no praise to you, but you command praise because of what does in you live.

Then, don't thank him for that which he does write (say) about your beauty & virtue, since you yourself are paying what he should have paid to you (that is, by writing praise about your beauty & virtue, he is not adding anything in your worth, rather, being such a virtuous & beautiful subject for his poem, you yourself are lending worth to his verse).

Sonnet 80

O, how I faint when I of you do write,
Knowing a better spirit doth use your name,
And in the praise thereof spends all his might,
To make me tongue-tied, speaking of your fame!

But since your worth (wide as the ocean is)
The humble as the proudest sail doth bear,
My saucy bark, inferior far to his,
On your broad main doth wilfully appear.

Your shallowest help will hold me up afloat,
While he upon your soundless deep doth ride;
Or, being wrecked, I am a worthless boat,
He of tall building, and of goodly pride:

Then if he thrive, and I be cast away,
The worst was this; - my love was my decay.

Explanation:

O, how I feel discouraged (faint) when I write about you, knowing that a better poet is also writing about you (a better spirit does use your name), and spends all his might in praising you, to make me tongue-tied in speaking about your fame!

But since your worth is wide like ocean, still humble in which proudest sail do bear, though my saucy bark is far inferior to his (other poet's) bark, but willfully do appear on your course.

Your slightest (shallowest) help will hold me up afloat, while he (other poet) does ride upon your unfathomed depth (soundless deep); or I, being wrecked, am a worthless boat, and he is like tall building, and of goodly (fine & ample) pride.

Then if he thrives (flourishes), and I am cast away, the worst was this; - my love was the reason of my decay.

Sonnet 81

Or I shall live your epitaph to make,
Or you survive when I in earth am rotten;
From hence your memory death cannot take,
Although in me each part will be forgotten.

Your name from hence immortal life shall have,
Though I, once gone, to all the world must die:
The earth can yield me but a common grave,
When you entombed in men's eyes shall lie.

Your monument shall be my gentle verse,
Which eyes not yet created shall o'er-read;
And tongues to be, your being shall rehearse,
When all the breathers of this world are dead;

You still shall live (such virtue hath my pen)
Where breath most breathes, - even in the mouths of men.

Explanation:

Whether I shall survive you (live to write your epitaph), or you survive when I am rotten in the earth, but the death can not take away your memory from hence (from now on), although I will be forgotten completely (in me each part will be forgotten).

From now onwards (from hence) your name shall have immortal life (shall live for ever), although I, once gone, shall die to all the world (I, once died, shall be forgotten completely): the earth can concede (yield) me but a common (ordinary) grave, whereas you shall live in men's eyes (you shall entombed lie in men's eye).

Your memory shall live in my gentle verse (my gentle poem shall be your monument), which shall be read again and again (over read) by the eyes of future generations (eyes not yet created), and which shall be repeated (rehearsed) by tongues of generations to come (tongues to be), when all the living ones of this generation (breathers of this world) are dead.

My pen (writings) has such quality (virtue) that you still shall live even in the mouths of men, where breath most breathes (that is, my poem has such quality that it will make you & your beauty live for ever in stories told by men from one generations to another generation).

Sonnet 82

I grant thou wert not married to my muse,
And there may'st without attaint o'erlook
The dedicated words which writers use
Of their fair subject, blessing every book.

Thou art as fair in knowledge as in hue,
Finding thy worth a limit past my praise;
And therefore art enforced to seek anew
Some fresher stamp of the time-bettering days.

And do so, love; yet when they have devis'd
What strained touches rhetoric can lend,
Thou truly fair wert truly sympathiz'd
In true plain words, by thy true-telling friend,

And their gross painting might be better us'd
Where cheeks need blood; in thee it is abus'd.

Explanation:

I grant that you were not married to my muse, and that you may, without disgracing (without attaint) overlook the dedicated words (words written in dedication), which writers use about their fair subject for blessing their every book.

Being as fair in knowledge as in looks (hue), and finding your worth much more than my praise, you are, therefore, enforced (compelled) to seek anew some fresher poet, who is bettered by advanced time, to write about you (some fresher stamp of the time-bettering days).

And, my love, do so; yet, you will find that when they (other poet of bettered time) have written false and showy (rhetoric) poems about you, which the exaggeration (strained touches) can produce; however, you, who is truly fair, were truly represented only in true & plain words of mine, your true-telling friend.

Their (other poets') exaggerated poems (gross paintings) might be good (might be better used) in praise of someone, who is not so beautiful as you (where cheek needs blood), but for you it is misplaced (abused).

Sonnet 83

I never saw that you did painting need,
And therefore to your fair no painting set.
I found, or thought I found, you did exceed
The barren tender of a poet's debt:

And therefore have I slept in your report
That you yourself, being extant, well might show
How far a modern quill doth come too short,
Speaking of worth, what worth in you doth grow.

This silence for my sin you did impute,
Which shall be most my glory; being dumb;
For I impair not beauty being mute,
When others would give life, and bring a tomb.

There lives more life in one of your fair eyes
Than both your poets can in praise devise.

Explanation:

I never felt (saw) that you need any ornament of praise (painting), and therefore, I have never praised your fair beauty. I found, or thought I found, that you did far exceed the barren praise offering of any poet's musing (you did exceed the barren tender of a poet's debt).

And therefore, I have lazily slept, and kept silent in praising you (slept in your report), thinking that you yourself, being extant (existing right here), might show much better than an ordinary reed (modern quill) would, that comes too short in praising the worth, which does in you grow.

You imputed (ascribed) my this silence as my sin, but, which, being dump, shall be my most glory, as, remaining silent, I am not impairing (reducing) your beauty, while others (other poets), by attempting to praise you, have, in fact, reduced your glory (would give life, and bring a tomb).

There exist much more beauty (lives more life) even in one of your fair eyes than whatever both your poets (i.e. me & others) could write (devise) in your praise.

Sonnet 84

Who is it that says most? Which can say more
Than this rich praise, - that you alone are you?
In whose confine immured is the store
Which should example where your equal grew?

Lean penury within that pen doth dwell,
That to his subject lends not some small glory;
But he that writes of you, if he can tell
That you are you, so dignifies his story,

Let him but copy what in you is writ,
Not making worse what nature made so clear,
And such a counterpart shall fame his wit,
Making his style admired everywhere.

You to your beauteous blessings add a curse,
Being fond on praise, which makes your praises worse.

Explanation:

Who is it that says most, which can say better (more) than this rich praise, "that you alone are you"? In whom, the treasure is immured (confined), exemplifying growth equal (parallel) to yours?

Extreme poverty (lean penury) dwells in that pen, which do not land some small glory to his subject; but he who writes of you, and if he can tell that "you are you", is able to dignify his writing (story).

Let him but (just) copy what is written in you, not making worse what Nature has made so clear, and such a counterpart (mere copy) alone shall fame his skill (wit), making his style admired everywhere (such unparallel is your beauty).

By being fond on praise, you add a curse to your beauteous blessing, which makes your praise worse (that is, you do possess such beauteous blessing of beauty that you need no praise, but by being fond on praise you add a curse to it, which makes your praise worse).

Sonnet 85

My tongue-tied muse in manners holds her still,
While comments of your praise, richly compil'd,
Reserve their character with golden quill,
And precious phrase by all the muses fil'd,

I think good thoughts, whilst other write good words,
And, like unlettered clerk, still cry 'Amen'
To every hymn that able spirit affords,
In polished form of well-refined pen.

Hearing you praised, I say, `Tis so, tis true',
And to the most of praise add something more;
But that is in my thought, whose love to you,
Though words come hindmost, holds his rank before.

Then others for the breath of words respect,
Me for my dumb thoughts, speaking in effect.

Explanation:

My polite, tongue-tied muse holds her in silence, while all other muses (all other poets) comments your praise in richly composed precious phrase, and reserve their character with golden quill.

I think good thoughts, whilst others write good words, and still, like uneducated (unlettered) clerk, I say "Amen" to every poem (hymn) that your able spirit is worthy of, written in polished form by other's well-refined pen (that able spirit affords in polished form of well-refined pen).

Hearing you praised, I say, "It is so, it is true", and add something more to the most of praise, but that "something more" is in my thought, for you which holds rank before the words of others that come hindmost (that is, I add something more to your praise, but that "something more" lies (is contained) in my thought, which is more important and dear to you than the words of others that comes thereafter).

So, then, respect others for the sound of their words (breath of words), and respect me for my dump thoughts, speaking in silence (speaking in effect).

Sonnet 86

Was it the proud full sail of his great verse,
Bound for the prize of all-too-precious you,
That did my ripe thoughts in my brain inhearse,
Making their tomb the womb wherein they grew?

Was it his spirit, by spirits taught to write
Above a mortal pitch, that struck me dead?
No, neither he, nor his compeers by night
Giving him aid, my virtue astonished.

He, nor that affable familiar ghost
Which nightly gulls him with intelligence,
As victors, of my silence cannot boast;
I was not sick of any fear from thence.

But when your countenance fil'd up his line,
Then lack'd I matter; that enfeebled mine.

Explanation:

Was it the proud full sail of his (other poet's) great verse, bound for the prize of all-too-precious you, that did entomb (bury) my ripe thoughts in my brain, the womb wherein they grew, making that womb itself their (i.e. my ripe thoughts') tomb?

Was it his spirit, taught to write on perishable papers (above a mortal pitch) by other spirits of unseen world, that struck me dead? No, neither he (i.e. other poet), nor his companion spirits (compeers) helping him by night, has stunned (astonished) my virtue.

Neither he (i.e. other poet), nor that friendly (affable) familiar ghost which nightly tricks (gulls) him with intelligence, cannot boast for making me silent (as victor of my silence), and I was not sick of any fear coming from there.

But, when the sign of approval on your face (your countenance) filled up his line (i.e. other poet's poem), then no matter was left with me, and that made me feeble (that is, but when I seen the approval on your face for him (i.e. for other poet), then nothing was left with me, and that made me almost collapsed).

Sonnet 87

Farewell! Thou art too dear for my possessing,
And like enough thou know'st thy estimate:
The charter of thy worth gives thee releasing;
My bonds in thee are all determinate.

For how do I hold thee but by thy granting?
And for that riches where is my deserving?
The cause of this fair gift in me is wanting,
And so my patent back again is swerving.

Thyself thou gav'st, thy own worth then not knowing,
Or me, to whom thou gavest it, else mistaking;
So thy great gift, upon misprision growing,
Comes home again, on better judgment making.

Thus have I had thee, as a dream doth flatter,
In sleep a king, but, waking, no such matter.

Explanation:

Good bye (farewell)! You are too dear for my possession, and as you know enough about your worth, the privilege (charter) of your worth itself sets you free (gives you release), my all bonds (all rights) upon you are ended (determinate).

For how can I hold you without your permission (granting), and where is my deserving for that riches which dwell in you? (That is I do not deserve those riches which dwell in you). The deservedness (cause) for this fair gift of you is wanting in me, and so, I am returning back (swerving back) my privilege (patent) upon you.

You yourself then gave your own worth to me without knowing enough, or you might have given it to me, mistaking me for someone else; so, your great gift that was mistakenly given (misprision growing) to me, comes back to you (comes home) again on my better judgment.

Thus, I have had you, as like in flattering dream; in sleep (while dreaming of having your gift) I was a king, but upon awaking, nothing exist of that sort (no such matter).

Sonnet 88

When thou shalt be dispos'd to set me light,
And place my merit in the eye of scorn,
Upon thy side against myself I'll fight,
And prove thee virtuous, though thou art forsworn:

With mine own weakness being best acquainted,
Upon thy part I can set down a story
Of faults concealed, wherein I am attainted;
That thou, in losing me, shall win much glory:

And I by this will be a gainer too;
For bending all my loving thoughts on thee,
The injuries that to myself I do,
Doing thee vantage, double-vantage me.

Such is my love, to thee I so belong,
That for thy right myself will bear all wrong.

Explanation:

When you shall be disposed to set me light, and look upon my merit with the scornful eye (place my merit in the eye of scorn), I will fight upon your side against myself, and shall prove you virtuous (faultless), though you are forsworn.

Being best acquainted with my own weakness, I can set down a story in your favor about my concealed (hidden) faults wherein I am attainted (guilty), and shall prove that, in losing me, you shall win much glory (that is, I shall prove that I am not worth keeping, and by leaving me you shall win much glory).

And by doing so I too shall be a gainer, as, by bending all my loving thoughts on you, the injuries that I inflict on myself for benefiting you (for doing you vantage) shall double-vantage me.

Such is my love and to you I so belong, that for your right (benefit) I shall bear all wrong (harm).

Sonnet 89

Say that thou didst forsake me for some fault,
And I will comment upon that offence:
Speak of my lameness, and I straight will halt;
Against thy reasons making no defence.

Thou canst not, love, disgrace me half so ill,
To set a form upon desired change,
As I'll myself disgrace: knowing thy will,
I will acquaintance strangle, and look strange;

Be absent from thy walks, and in my tongue
Thy sweet-beloved name no more shall dwell;
Lest I (too much profane) should do it wrong,
And haply of our old acquaintance tell.

For thee, against myself I'll vow debate,
For I must ne'er love him whom thou dost hate.

Explanation:

Just say that you did forsake (leave) me for my some fault (failing), and I shall comment upon that my offence by speaking about my own lameness (weakness), and I will stand still (halt) making no defence against your reasons.

O Love, you can not disgrace me half so much as I would disgrace myself upon knowing your such wish, to set a form upon desired change; I will kill (strangle) our acquaintance, and look (pretend) stranger.

I will remain absent from the ways upon which you walk, and I will no more bring your sweet-beloved name on my tongue, otherwise, I, being too much profane, may do wrong of haply (by chance) telling about our old acquaintance.

For you (i.e. to defend you), I will vow to debate against myself, as, I must never love him (i.e. me) whom you do hate.

Sonnet 90

Then hate me when thou wilt; if ever, now;
Now while the world is bent my deeds to cross.
Join with the spite of fortune, make me bow,
   And do not drop in for an after-loss:

Ah! do not, when my heart hath 'scaped this sorrow,
   Come in the rearward of a conquer'd woe;
   Give not a windy night, a rainy morrow,
   To linger out a purposed overthrow.

If thou wilt leave me, do not leave me last,
When other petty griefs have done their spite,
   But in the onset come; so shall I taste
   At first the very worse of fortune's might;

And other strains of woe, which now seem woe,
   Compared with loss of thee will not seem so.

Explanation:

If you ever wish to hate me, hate me now; now while the world has bent deeds to cross. Join the blow (spite) of misfortune and make me bow, but do not come last to blow me for an after-loss.

Ah, do not come in the rearward of already conquered woe, when my heart has escaped (overcome) this sorrow; don't give an additional blow (a windy night, a rainy morrow) to linger out (prolong) a planed (purposed) overthrow.

If you wish to leave me, don't leave me last, when other petty pains (griefs) have done their blows (spites), but leave me in the onset (i.e. in the beginning of misfortune itself), so that I shall taste at first (i.e. as first blow) the very worse might (strength) of misfortune.

And compared with the loss of you, other strains (blows) of those woes that now itself are woes will not seem so hard.

191

Sonnet 91

Some glory in their birth, some in their skill,
Some in their wealth, some in their body's force;
Some in their garments, though new-fangled ill;
Some in their hawks and hounds, some in their horse:

And every humour hath his adjunct pleasure,
Wherein it finds a joy above the rest;
But these particulars are not my measure,
All these I better in one general best.

Thy love is better than high birth to me,
Richer than wealth, prouder than garments' cost,
Of more delight than hawks or horses be;
And, having thee, of all men's pride I boast.

Wretched in this alone, that thou mayst take
All this away, and me most wretched make.

Explanation:

Some men glory in their high birth, some glory in their talent (skill), some glory in their wealth, some in their physical strength (body's force), some in their fashionably ugly (new-fangled ill) cloths, and some in their hawks, hounds and horse.

Every disposition (humour) has its special added (adjunct) pleasure, wherein it finds a joy more than the rest, but these particulars are not my measure, for me something else (one general best) is better than all these.

For me, your love is better than high birth, richer than wealth, prouder than cost of garments, of more delight than hawks or horse, and, I boast in having you, the pride of all men.

I am fearful (wretched) about only one thing that some day you may take all these away from me, and make me most wretched (that is, my only fear is, some day you may go away from me, and make me completely wretched).

Sonnet 92

But do thy worst to steal thy self away,
For term of life, thou art assured mine;
And life no longer than thy love will stay,
For it depends upon that love of thine.

Then need I not to fear the worst of wrongs,
When in the least of them, my life hath end.
I see a better state to me belongs
Than that which on thy humour doth depend;

Thou canst not vex me with inconstant mind,
Since that my life on thy revolt doth lie.
O, what a happy title do I find,
Happy to have thy love, happy to die!

But what's so blessed-fair that fears no blot?
- Thou mayst be false, and yet I know it not.

Explanation:

Do whatever you want to steal your self (love) away from me, for this life (for term of life) you are assured mine; and my life will not last longer than the time your love stays in my life, as, my life depends on your love.

Then I need not fear the worst of wrongs, as, on your love leaving me (in the least of them) my life will have the end. I see that, in that case (i.e. in case of my death upon you leaving me), I will be in better state than the present state, which depend on your whims (humour).

You can not annoy (vex) me with inconstancy (inconstant mind), since that my life (i.e. my life after my death) does lie on your revolt. O, what a happy title I have found, "Happy to have your love, happy to die"!

But what is so blessed-fair state that fears no blot? - You may be false, and yet I do not know it (that is, but, you may be false and I do not know it, is, for me, the blessed-fair state that fear no blemish).

Sonnet 93

So shall I live, supposing thou art true,
Like a deceived husband; so love's face
May still seem love to me, though alter'd new;
Thy looks with me, thy heart in other place;

For there can live no hatred in thine eye,
Therefore in that I cannot know thy change.
In many's looks the false heart's history
Is writ, in moods and frowns and wrinkles strange;

But heaven in thy creation did decree
That in thy face sweet love should ever dwell,
Whate'er thy thoughts or thy heart's workings be,
Thy looks should nothing thence but sweetness tell.

How like Eve's apple doth thy beauty grow,
If thy sweet virtue answer not thy show.

Explanation:

Like a deceived husband, I shall live believing (supposing) that you are true, so that your (love's) face may still seem love to me, though it is changed (altered new); your looks is with me, but your heart is with other (in other place).

As, in your eyes no hatred can live, therefore in that I cannot see your change, unlike many in whose looks the false heart's entire history is written, in moods, in frowns and in strange wrinkles.

But, while creating you, the heaven did decree (order) that in your face sweet love shall ever dwell; whatever may be your thought, or whatever may be your heart's feelings (heart's workings), but your looks shall show (tell) therefrom (thence) nothing except the sweetness.

How like Eve's apple does your beauty grow, if your sweet virtue answer (respond) rather than your show (looks)!

Sonnet 94

They that have power to hurt, and will do none,
That do not do the thing they most do show,
Who, moving others, are themselves as stone,
Unmoved, cold, and to temptation slow;

They rightly do inherit heaven's graces,
And husband nature's riches from expense;
They are the lords and owners of their faces,
Others but stewards of their excellence.

The summer's flower is to the summer sweet
Though to itself it only live and die;
But if that flower with base infection meet,
The basest weed outbraves his dignity:

For sweetest things turn sourest by their deeds:
Lilies that fester smell far worse than weeds.

Explanation:

Those who have power to hurt, but will hurt none, those who do not do those things which appear in them most, those who, moving others, are themselves like stone, unmoved, cold, and very slow towards temptations;

They rightly do inherit Heaven's grace, and guard (husband) the Nature's riches from misuse (expense); they are the lords and owners of their faces, others are but stewards of their excellence.

The summer's flower is sweet to the summer, though to itself only it lives and dies; but if that flower meet with base infection, it becomes worst than even basest weed (the basest weed outbrave its dignity):

Because, the sweetest thing turns to be the sourest by their (bad) deeds, like lilies (lotuses) when they fester (decay) they smell far worse than weeds.

Sonnet 95

How sweet and lovely dost thou make the shame,
Which, like a canker in the fragrant rose,
Doth spot the beauty of thy budding name!
O, in what sweets dost thou thy sins enclose!

That tongue that tells the story of thy days,
Making lascivious comments on thy sport,
Cannot dispraise but in a kind of praise:
Naming thy name blesses an ill report.

O, what a mansion have those vices got
Which for their habitation chose out thee!
Where beauty's veil doth cover every blot,
And all things turn to fair, that eyes can see!

Take heed, dear heart, of this large privilege;
The hardest knife ill-used doth lose his edge.

Explanation:

How sweet and lovely you do make the same, which like a canker (disease of plant) in fragrant (smelling) rose, does spot the beauty of your budding name! O, in what sweets you do hide (enclose) your sins!

That tongue which tells the story of your days, making lascivious (sexy) comments about your activities (sport), cannot dispraise you but it seems like a kind of praise, and just by mentioning your name it blesses (glorifies) an ill report.

O, what a mansion (home) have those vices got, which chose out you for their habitation! Where beauty's veil do cover every blot (taint), and all things turn to beauty (fair), that eyes can see!

O, dear heart, take heed (beware) of this large privilege; the sharpest (hardest) knife when ill-used (wrongly used) does lose its edge.

Sonnet 96

Some say thy fault is youth, some wantonness,
Some say thy grace is youth and gentle sport;
Both grace and faults are loved of more and less:
Thou mak'st faults graces that to thee resort.

As on the finger of a throned Queen
The basest jewel will be well esteem'd;
So are those errors that in thee are seen
To truths translated, and for true things deem'd.

How many lambs might the stern wolf betray,
If like a lamb he could his looks translate!
How many gazers might'st thou lead away,
If thou wouldst use the strength of all thy state!

But do not so; I love thee in such sort,
As thou being mine, mine is thy good report.

Explanation:

Some say that youth is your fault, some say wantonness (sexual immorality), and some say that your grace is youth and gentle gestures (sport); your grace and faults are both loved more and less, you make faults into graces that in you reside (that to thee resort).

As like the basest jewel on the finger of a throned Queen will be esteemed, so are those errors that are visible (seen) in you, get translated into truth, and are deemed for true things.

How many lambs the stern wolf might betray, if the wolf could change (translate) his looks to appear like lamb! In the same way, how many gazers (i.e. people who gaze upon you) you might lead astray (away), if you would use all your strength (the strength of all your state)!

But don't do so; I love you in such a way (in such sort) that, as you being mine, to my eye you ever command the good report (that is, but don't do so, because, I love you to such an extent that for me your report is always good).

Sonnet 97

How like a winter hath my absence been
From thee, the pleasure of the fleeting year!
What freezing have I felt, what dark days seen!
What old December's bareness everywhere!

And yet this time removed was summer's time,
The teeming autumn, big with rich increase,
Bearing the wanton burden of the prime,
Like widow'd wombs after their lords' decease;

Yet this abundant issue seem'd to me
But hope of orphans, and unfather'd fruit;
For summer and his pleasures wait on thee,
And, thou away, the very birds are mute;

Or, if they sing, 'tis with so dull a cheer,
That leaves look pale, dreading the winter's near.

Explanation:

How, like a winter, has my absence been from you, the pleasure of the fleeting year! What freezing cold have I felt, what dark days have I seen! What a bareness everywhere of old December!

And yet this separation time (time removed) was summer's time, the teeming (full) autumn, big with rich increase, bearing wanton burden of prime (youth's sex desire's burden), like widowed wombs after their husband's death (their lord's decease);

Yet this abundant issue seemed to me but like hope of orphans, and un-fathered child (fruit), because summer and his pleasures wait on you, and, you being away, all birds are silent (mute);

Or, if they sing, it is in so dull a voice (with so dull a cheer), that leaves look pale, dreading (fearing) the winter is near.

Sonnet 98

From you have I been absent in the spring,
When proud-pied April, dress'd in all his trim,
Hath put a spirit of youth in everything,
That heavy Saturn laugh'd and leap'd with him.

Yet nor the lays of birds, nor the sweet smell
Of different flowers in odour and in hue,
Could make me any summer's story tell,
Or from their proud lap pluck them where they grew:

Nor did I wonder at the lilies white,
Nor praise the deep vermilion in the rose;
They were but sweet, but figures of delight,
Drawn after you, you pattern of all those.

Yet seemed it winter still, and you, away,
As with your shadow I with these did play.

Explanation:

I have been absent from you in the spring, when proudly colorful (proud-pied) April, dressed in all his beauty has put a spirit of youth in everything, that even heavy Saturn (Saturn is considered to be slow, heavy and sad) laughed and leaped with him (with April).

Yet, neither the songs (lays) of birds, nor the sweet smell of beautifully colored and fully odoured flowers (flowers in odour and in hue) could make me tell summer's happy story, or make me pluck them from their proud lap where they grow:

Nor did I wonder at the beautiful whiteness of lilies, nor praise the deep vermilion (bright redness) in the rose; they were sweet and figures of delight, but drawn after you, you being the pattern of all those.

Yet, still it (i.e. April) seemed winter, and you, being away, I did play with them, but, as if playing with your shadow.

Sonnet 99

The forward violet thus did I chide; -
Sweet Thief, whence didst thou steal thy sweet that smells,
If not from my love's breath? The purple pride
Which on thy soft cheek for complexion dwells,

In my love's veins thou hast too grossly dyed,
The lily I condemned for thy hand.
And buds of marjoram had stol'n thy hair:
The roses fearfully on thorns did stand,

One blushing shame, another white despair;
A third, nor red nor white, had stol'n of both,
And to his robbery had annex'd thy breath;
But for his theft, in pride of all his growth
A vengeful canker eat him up to death.

More flowers I noted, yet I none could see,
But sweet or colour it had stolen from thee.

Explanation:

Thus I did chide the forward violet; "Sweet thief, from where did you steal your sweet that smells, if not from my love's breath? The purple pride, which, dwells on your soft cheek for complexion, has dyed (colored) itself too grossly in my love's veins.

I condemned the lily for your hand (i.e. for steeling your hand). The buds of marjoram had stolen your hair, and the roses did stand fearfully on thorns.

One (i.e. red rose) had stolen blushing shame, another (i.e. white lily) had stolen white despair, a third one, neither red nor white (i.e. rose of other color) had stolen the both, and to his robbery has attached (annexed) your breath (smell); but, for this theft, when he is in pride for all his growth, a vengeful canker (plant disease) eat him up to death.

Many more flowers I noted, yet I could see none, who has not stolen sweet smell or beautiful color from you!

Sonnet 100

Where art thou, Muse, that thou forgett'st so long
To speak of that which gives thee all thy might?
Spend'st thou thy fury on some worthless song,
Darkening thy power, to lend base subjects light?

Return, forgetful Muse, and straight redeem
In gentle numbers time so idly spent;
Sing to the ear that doth thy lays esteem,
And gives thy pen both skill and argument.

Rise, resty Muse, my love's sweet face survey,
If Time have any wrinkle graven there;
If any, be a satire to decay,
And make Time's spoils despised everywhere.

Give my love fame faster than Time wastes life;
So thou prevent'st his scythe and crooked knife.

Explanation:

O Muse, where are you, that you forget so long to speak (write) about that which gives you all your might? Why you spend your vehemence (fury) on writing some worthless song, darkening your power to lend light to base subject?

O forgetful Muse, come back, and by writing gentle poems (numbers), straight redeem (recover) the time you spent so idly; sing to the ear that esteem your lays (songs), and gives your pen both skill and subject (argument).

O Muse, rise from your rest, and observe (survey) my love's sweet face, whether Time have engraved any wrinkle there, and if it has, then ridicule it (i.e. the Time) to decay, and make Time's spoils (spoiling effects) despised everywhere.

O muse, give my love fame faster than the Time wastes life, so that, you can prevent Time's scythe and crooked knife from cutting my love's beauty & youth.

Sonnet 101

O truant Muse, what shall be thy amends
For thy neglect of truth in beauty dyed?
Both truth and beauty on my love depends;
So dost thou too, and therein dignified.

Make answer, Muse: wilt thou not haply say,
"Truth needs no colour with his colour fixed,
Beauty no pencil, beauty's truth to lay;
But best is best, if never intermix'd?" -

Because he needs no praise, wilt thou be dumb?
Excuse not silence so; for it lies in thee
To make him much outlive a gilded tomb,
And to be praised of ages yet to be.

Then do thy office, Muse; I teach you how
To make him seem long hence as he shows now.

Explanation:

O truant (who stays away without permission) Muse, what shall you do to redeem your neglect of ornamenting the truth with beauty? Both truth and beauty depends on my beloved, and so you too, dignified by writing about my love (therein dignified).

Give answer, Mush: will you not haply say "Truth needs no colour as its colour is fixed, beauty needs no pencil to establish (lay) its truth; but best is best, if never intermixed?"

Because my beloved needs no praise, will you remain silent (dumb)? Don't give such excuses to justify your silence; as, it lies in you to make my beloved immortal (much outlive a gilded tomb), and to make my beloved to be praised by generations to come.

Then do your work (office), Muse; I teach you how to make my beloved look ever (seem long hence) as he looks (shows) now (that is, I teach you how to make truth and beauty of my beloved immortal in the eyes of generations to come).

Sonnet 102

My love is strengthen'd, though more weak in seeming;
I love not less, though less the show appear;
That love is merchandised whose rich esteeming
The owner's tongue doth publish everywhere.

Our love was new, and then but in the spring,
When I was wont to greet it with my lays;
As Philomel in summer's front doth sing,
And stops her pipe in growth of riper days:

Not that the summer is less pleasant now
Than when her mournful hymns did hush the night,
But that wild music burthens every bough,
And sweets grown common lose their dear delight.

Therefore, like her, I sometimes hold my tongue,
Because I would not dull you with my song.

Explanation:

My love is strengthened (became more strong), though it seems more weak (weak in seeming); I love not less, though it appears less (less the show appear); that love becomes a thing of merchandise (is merchandised) whose rich value (esteeming) is published everywhere by its owner himself (owner's tongue).

When our love was new, and was in the spring (when our love was young), I used to greet it with my poems (lays); as Philomel (the nightingale) does sing in summer's front (i.e. in the beginning of summer) and stops her singing (pipe) during the later (riper) days.

It is not that the summer is less pleasant now than the time when nightingale's sad songs (mournful hymns) quieted (hushed) the night, but that when wild music burdens every bough (branch), and when sweets become very common, they lose their dear delight.

Therefore, like nightingale, I sometimes hold my tongue (i.e. become silent) because I would not like to dull you with my words (song).

Sonnet 103

Alack! what poverty my Muse brings forth,
That having such a scope to show her pride,
The argument, all bare, is of more worth,
Than when it hath my added praise beside.

O blame me not if I no more can write!
Look in thy glass, and there appears a face
That over-goes my blunt invention quite,
Dulling my lines, and doing me disgrace.

Were it not sinful, then, striving to mend,
To mar the subject that before was well?
For to no other pass my verses tend,
Than of your graces and your gifts to tell;

And more, much more, than in my verse can sit,
Your own glass shows you, when you look in it.

Explanation:

Alack! What poverty my Muse brings forth, that also when having such a scope to show her (i.e. my love's) pride! Even entirely bare argument (subject), seems of more worth, than when it has my added praise beside!

O, blame me not if I no more can write! Rather, look in your mirror (glass), and there you will see a face appearing (i.e. your own face) that goes quite far than my edgeless praise (blunt invention), dulling my lines (poem), and doing me disgrace.

Were it not sinful, then, to damage (mar) the subject that was already well (that before was well), by striving to mend (improve) it? As, no other purpose my verses serve, than to tell your graces and your gifts.

When you look in your mirror (glass) it will show you more, much more beauty than my verse can tell (than in my verse can sit).

Sonnet 104

To me, fair friend, you never can be old,
For as you were when first your eye I eyed,
Such seems your beauty still. Three winters' cold
Have from the forests shook three summers' pride;

Three beauteous springs to yellow autumn turn'd
In process of the seasons have I seen;
Three April perfumes in three hot Junes burn'd,
Since first I saw you fresh, which yet are green.

Ah! Yet doth beauty, like a dial-hand,
Steal from his figure, and no pace perceived:
So your sweet hue, which methinks still doth stand,
Hath motion, and mine eye may be deceived.

For fear of which, hear this, thou age unbred,
Ere you were born, was beauty's summer dead.

Explanation:

O my fair (beauteous) friend, to me, you never can be old, because, your beauty looks still the same as you were when first I eyed your eye. Three winter's cold have shook three summer's leaves (pride) from the forests;

Three beauteous springs turned into yellow autumn, in the process of the seasons, I have seen, three April perfumes have been burned in three hot Junes, since I first saw you fresh, which yet is as young (green).

Ah! Yet beauty does, like a dial-hand (clock-hand), steals from itself (from his figure), but time seems to be standing still (no pace is perceived), so is your sweet beauty (hue), which, though methinks does stand still, has motion (i.e. is aging), and my eye may be deceived.

For fear of which, O generation yet unborn, hear this, before (ere) you were born, beauty's peak (beauty's summer) was dead when my beloved died (that is, O generations yet unborn, hear this, you all will never see what beauty's peak can be, as, before you were born, the beauty's peak was dead with the death of my beloved - in my beloved, the beauty has used itself up).

Sonnet 105

Let not my love be call'd idolatry,
Nor my beloved as an idol show,
Since all alike my songs and praises be,
To one, of one, still such, and ever so.

Kind is my love to-day, to-morrow kind,
Still constant in a wondrous excellence;
Therefore my verse, to constancy confined,
One thing expressing, leaves out difference.

Fair, kind, and true, is all my argument,
Fair, kind, and true, varying to other words;
And in this change is my invention spent,
Three themes in one, which wondrous scope affords.

Fair, kind, and true, have often lived alone,
Which three, till now, never kept seat in one.

Explanation:

Let not my love be called idolatry (idol worshiping), nor my beloved be called just as an idol (as an idol show), since all my songs and praises are all alike, dedicated to one, of one, still the same, and ever so.

My love is kind to-day, is to-morrow kind, and is always constant in a wondrous excellence, therefore, my verses are confined to constancy, expressing one thing (i.e. my love) and leaving out all others.

Fair, kind, and true, is all my subject (argument) for writing; fair, kind, and true is expressed in different words (varying to other words), and in this change (i.e. in expressing the same thing in different words) my entire creative skill (invention) is spent; three themes in one person, which provides (affords) wondrous scope for writing.

Beauty (fair), kindness (kind), and truth (true) have often lived alone (separately), but, these three virtues have never lived together in one person, except my beloved (till now, never kept seat in one).

Sonnet 106

When in the chronicle of wasted time
I see descriptions of the fairest wights,
And beauty making beautiful old rhyme,
In praise of ladies dead and lovely knights,

Then in the blazon of sweet beauty's best,
Of hand, of foot, of lip, of eye, of brow,
I see their antique pen would have express'd
Even such a beauty as you master now.

So all their praises are but prophecies
Of this our time, all you prefiguring;
And, for they look'd but with divining eyes,
They had not skill enough your worth to sing:

For we, which now behold these present days,
Have eyes to wonder, but lack tongues to praise.

Explanation:

When I see descriptions of fairest people in historical records of past misspent (wasted) time, and when I see the beauty (i.e. fine poet) making beautiful old poems in praise of ladies dead and lovely knights.

Then I see that in the blazon (display) of sweet beauty's best of hand, foot, lip, eye, or brow, the past poets' antique pen have expressed such a beauty as you possess now.

So all their (antique poets') praises are but prophecies of this our time, they all imagining you beforehand, and as they seen (looked) you but with divining (future seeing) eyes, they had not enough skill to describe (sing) your worth fully (that is, finest description of the best of past beauties fell far short to describe your beauty, such, never-happened-before, is the beauty of my love).

We, who now behold you in these present days, have eyes to wonder, but lack tongues to praise (that is, we now behold you alive in these present days, and feel amazed (wondered) seeing your such beauteous beauty, but are not able to praise it enough by tongue).

Sonnet 107

Not mine own fears, nor the prophetic soul
Of the wide world, dreaming on things to come,
Can yet the lease of my true love control,
Supposed as forfeit to a confined doom.

The mortal moon has her eclipse endured,
And the sad augurs mock their own presage;
Uncertainties now grown themselves assured,
And peace proclaims olives of endless age.

Now with the drops of this most balmy time
My love looks fresh, and Death to me subscribes,
Since spite of him I'll live in this poor rhyme,
While he insults o'er dull and speechless tribes.

And thou in this shall find thy monument,
When tyrants' crests and tombs of brass are spent.

Explanation:

Not my own fears, nor the prophetic soul of wide world, who dreams (predicts) on things to come, can yet control the life (lease) of my true love, supposed as forfeit (limited) to a confined doom.

The mortal moon has endured her eclipse, and the sad augurs (fortune tellers) mock on their own presage (prediction); uncertainties have now grown themselves into sureties, and olives of endless age proclaim peace.

Now with the drops of this most pleasant (balmy) time my love looks fresh, and the death submits (subscribes) to me, since, in spite of him (i.e. death) I will live in this humble poem (poor rhyme), while he (i.e. death) triumphs (insults) over-dull and ignorant people (speechless tribes).

And you, my love, shall find your monument in this poem, when tyrants' crests and tombs of brass are spent (that is, my love, memories of you and your beauty shall be preserved in this poem, when even tyrants' heads and long lasting tombs of brass are destroyed).

Sonnet 108

What's in the brain that ink may character,
Which hath not figured to thee my true spirit?
What's new to speak, what's new to register,
That may express my love, or thy dear merit?

Nothing, sweet boy, but yet, like prayers divine,
I must each day say o'er the very same;
Counting no old thing old, thou mine, I thine,
Even as when first I hallow'd thy fair name.

So that eternal love in love's fresh case
Weighs not the dust and injury of age,
Nor gives to necessary wrinkles place,
But makes antiquity for aye his page;

Finding the first conceit of love there bred,
Where time and outward form would show it dead.

Explanation:

What is in the mind that pen (ink) may write (character), which my true spirit has not illustrated (figured) to you? What is new there to speak, what is new there to register, that may express my love, or may express your dear merit?

Nothing, my beloved, but yet, like divine prayers, I must say over the very same every day, counting (treating) no old thing as old, "you mine, I yours", even as when I first hallowed (respected) your fair (beautiful) name.

So that, every time the eternal love weighs not the dust and injury of age, nor give place to necessary (unavoidable) wrinkles, but makes all these antiquity to approve (aye) the record (page) of love,

Finding the first conceit (metaphor) of love alive (bred) there, where the time and outward form would show it dead.

Sonnet 109

O, never say that I was false of heart,
Though absence seem'd my flame to qualify!
As easy might I from myself depart,
As from my soul, which in thy breast doth lie:

That is my home of love: if I have ranged,
Like him that travels, I return again;
Just to the time, not with the time exchanged, -
So that myself brings water for my stain.

Never believe, though in my nature reign'd
All frailties that besiege all kinds of blood,
That it could so preposterously be stain'd,
To leave for nothing all thy sum of good;

For nothing this wide universe I call,
Save thou, my rose; in it thou art my all.

Explanation:

O, never say that I was false of heart, though my absence from you seemed as if my flame to qualify! Departing form you is as like departing from myself, from my soul itself, which dwells in your breast (heart).

That (i.e. your heart) is my home of love, if I have gone here and there (ranged), like a traveler, I return again, exactly at the right time without wasting any time, so that I myself bring water (remedy) for my stain.

Though all weaknesses that are common to all people (that besiege all kinds of blood) ruled my nature, but never believe that my nature could be stained so absurdly, that it could make me leave all your sum of good for nothing.

Because, in this wide world I call nothing, except you, as my rose, and in this wide world you are my all and everything.

Sonnet 110

Alas, 'tis true, I have gone here and there,
And made myself a motley to the view,
Gored mine own thoughts, sold cheap what is most dear,
Made old offences of affection new.

Most true it is, that I have look'd on truth
Askance and strangely; but, by all above,
These blenches gave my heart another youth,
And worse essays proved thee my best of love.

Now all is done, have what shall have no end;
Mine appetite I never more will grind
On newer proof, to try an older friend,
A God in love, to whom I am confined.

Then give me welcome, next my heaven the best,
Even to thy pure and most most loving breast.

Explanation:

Alas, it is true that I have gone here and there and made myself a motley (a jester or a fool) in eyes of others, gored (spoiled) my own thoughts, sold cheap what is most precious (dear), and by making new friends offended old friends.

It is most (completely) true that I have looked on truth askance (with disdain) and strangely (like a stranger); but, above all, these blenches (unseemly actions) gave my heart new zeal for your love (another youth), and these worse experiences (essays) have proved that you are my best of love.

As, now all is done (gone), I have that (i.e. value for your love) which shall have no end; no more I will grind my appetite (lust) upon newer friend (proof), and will not try (betray) an older friend, you, a God in love, to whom now I am confined (faithful).

So, then, give me welcome in your pure and most most loving heart, which, for me, is heaven the best.

Sonnet 111

O, for my sake, do you with Fortune chide,
The guilty goddess of my harmful deeds,
That did not better for my life provide,
Than public means, which public manners breeds.

Thence comes it that my name receives a brand,
And almost thence my nature is subdued
To what it works in, like the dyer's hand:
Pity me then, and wish I were renew'd;

Whilst, like a willing patient, I will drink
Potions of eysell, against my strong infection;
No bitterness that I will bitter think,
Nor double penance, to correct correction.

Pity me then, dear friend, and I assure ye,
Even that your pity is enough to cure me.

Explanation:

O, for my sake, you do chide the fortune, the guilty goddess responsible for all my harmful deeds. The fortune has not provided anything better for my life, than a common (public) means, like all other ordinary people.

Thence (i.e. from fortune) it comes that my name receives a brand (i.e. bad name), and almost thence (i.e. by fortune) my nature is made subdued (commensurate) to my petty activities, as like the dyer's hand becomes tainted with the color he works with: then, pity me, and wish that I be transformed (renewed).

Whilst, like a willing patient, I will drink potions of eysell (I will willingly gulp any poison-like medicine, suffering), against my strong infection (i.e. to transform my reactive & self-despising inner nature), I will not think any bitterness (suffering) as bitter (condemnable), and am ready to undergo double penance (double self-punishment in repentance) to bring about required correction (transformation) in me.

Pity me then, my divine beloved (dear friend), and I assure you that your pity (your compassionate love) is enough to transform (cure) me.

Sonnet 112

Your love and pity doth the impression fill
Which vulgar scandal stamp'd upon my brow;
For what care I who calls me well or ill,
So you o'ergreen my bad, my good allow?

You are my all-the-world, and I must strive
To know my shames and praises from your tongue;
None else to me, nor I to none alive,
That my steel'd sense or changes, right or wrong.

In so profound abysm, I throw all care
Of others' voices, that my adder's sense
To critic and to flatter stopped are.
Mark how with my neglect I do dispense;-

You are so strongly in my purpose bred,
That all the world beside methinks are dead.

Explanation:

Your love and compassion does efface the scar (the impression fill) which the vulgar scandal has stamped upon my brow; when you so over-green (i.e. correct) my bad, and make my good flourish (allow), then, for what I should care, who calls me good or bad?

You are my all-the-world (my all & everything), and I must strive to know my shames (weaknesses) and praises (strengths) from your tongue; no one else is alive to me, nor I am alive to anyone else, let mine this insensitivity (steeled sense) or change be right or wrong.

I throw all care of others' voices in so profound abyss (abysm), that my ears (my adder's sense) to critic as well as to flatter are closed. Listen (mark) how I deal (do dispense) with mine this neglect:--

You are so strongly imbedded (bred) in my purpose (in my being, in my existence) that all the world around (beside) methinks dead (seems dead to me).

Sonnet 113

Since I left you, mine eye is in my mind;
And that which governs me to go about
Doth part his function, and is partly blind,
Seems seeing, but effectually is out;

For it no form delivers to the heart,
Of bird, of flower, or shape, which it doth latch;
Of his quick objects hath the mind no part,
Nor his own vision holds what it doth catch;

For if it see the rudest or gentlest sight,
The most sweet favour, or deformed'st creature,
The mountain or the sea, the day or night,
The crow, or dove, it shapes them to your feature.

Incapable of more, replete with you,
My most true mind thus maketh mine untrue.

Explanation:

Since I left you, my eye is in my mind; and my eye which directs my foot-steps (governs me) to go about is not doing his job (function), and is now partly blind, seems seeing but actually not.

For it delivers no form (image) to the heart, either of bird, or of flower, or of the shape which it see; and the mind also do not take part in seeing the objects that eye presents in quick succession, nor eye's own vision holds what it does focus upon.

Because, if it see the rudest or gentlest sight, the most sweet favour or most deformed creature, the mountain or the see, the day or the night, the crow or dove, it converts (shapes) them all to your feature (that is, my eye sees only you in all other sights or shapes).

And being replete (full) with you, and incapable of holding anything else, my most true mind thus makes my vision untrue.

Sonnet 114

Or whether doth my mind, being crown'd with you,
Drink up the Monarch's plague, this flattery,
Or whether shall I say, mine eye saith true,
And that your love taught it this alchemy,

To make of monsters and things indigest
Such cherubims as your sweet self resemble,
Creating every bad a perfect best,
As fast as objects to his beams assemble?

So, 'tis the first; 'tis flattery in my seeing,
And my great mind most kingly drinks it up:
Mine eye well knows what with his gust is 'greeing,
And to his palate doth prepare the cup:

If it be poisoned,' tis the lesser sin
That mine eye loves it, and doth first begin.

Explanation:

Whether my mind, being crowned with you, does drink up the Monarch's plague (i.e. insincere praise), this flattery, or should I say that my eye said true (shown truth), but your love taught my eye this alchemy (art of transmutation),

To transmute (make of) monsters and shapeless things into such cherubins (young angels) as your sweet self resemble, creating every bad into a perfect best, as fast as the object come in contact with eye's beams?

So, first of all, it is flattery in my view (seeing), and my great mind most kindly drinks it up (absorbs it without resistance): my eye well knows what my mind's sense of taste (gust) likes, and according to mental likings (palate) does prepare the cup (present the sight):-

If it (i.e. the cup) is poisoned with flattery, it is the lesser sin, as, my eye loves it, and does begin to drink it first.

Sonnet 115

Those lines that I before have writ, do lie;
Even those that said I could not love you dearer;
Yet then my judgment knew no reason why
My most full flame should afterwards burn clearer.

But reckoning time, whose million'd accidents
Creep in `twixt vows, and change decrees of kings,
Tan sacred beauty, blunt the sharp'st intents,
Divert strong minds to the course of altering things;

Alas! why, fearing of Time's tyranny,
Might I not then say "Now love I you best,"
When I was certain o'er uncertainty,
Crowning the present, doubting of the rest?'

Love is a babe; then might I not say so,
To give full growth to that which still doth grow?

Explanation:

Those lines that I have wrote before, do lie, even those lines that said I could not love you dearer, do lie; yet then my judgment knew no reason why my most full flame of love should burn still more clearer afterwards.

But, considering (reckoning) time, whose millions accidents nullify vows, change decrees (orders) of kings, tan (spoil) sacred beauty, blunt the sharpest intentions, and divert strong minds to the course of occurring changes (altering things),

Alas! Why, fearing of Time's this tyranny, when I was certain about uncertainty, crowning the present and ignoring the future (crowning the present, doubting of the rest), then I not say "Now I love you best"?

Why I not say then that my love is a babe in order to give full growth to that which still does grow? (In other words, that time I didn't say "Now I love you best", because I knew that still my love is like babe, which is still growing, so, in order to give full growth to my love, that time I didn't say, "Now I love you best").

Sonnet 116

Let me not to the marriage of true minds
Admit impediments. Love is not love
Which alters when it alteration finds,
Or bends with the remover to remove:

O, no; it is an ever-fixed mark,
That looks on tempests, and is never shaken;
It is the star to every wandering bark,
Whose worth's unknown, although his height be taken.

Love's not time's fool, though rosy lips and cheeks
Within his bending sickle's compass come;
Love alters not with his brief hours and weeks,
But bears it out even to the edge of doom.

If this be error and upon me proved,
I never writ, nor no man ever loved.

Explanation:

Let me not admit impediments to the marriage of true minds (that is, let me not admit that problems, personal flaws etc can spoil the marriage of true minds). Love is not love if it alters when it finds alteration in the other, or if it bends with the opposition or difficulties.

O, no; it is ever fixed mark, even while looking on the tempests it is never shaken; it is like the star (North Pole) to every wondering bark in the sea, unshaken and ever guiding, though it's worth is unknown.

Love is not a game of time (time's fool), though the time, with its sickle, can cut down the youth (rosy lips and cheeks), but love does not alter (change) with time's brief hours and weeks, and survives (bears it out) even to the edge of doom (doomsday).

If it is proved upon me that this is not true (error), then I have never written, and no one has ever loved.

Sonnet 117

Accuse me thus; that I have scanted all
Wherein I should your great deserts repay,
Forgot upon your dearest love to call,
Whereto all bonds do tie me day by day;

That I have frequent been with unknown minds,
And given to time your own dear-purchased right;
That I have hoisted sail to all the winds
Which should transport me farthest from your sight.

Book both my wilfulness and errors down,
And on just proof surmise accumulate,
Bring me within the level of your frown,
But shoot not at me in your waken'd hate:

Since my appeal says, I did strive to prove
The constancy and virtue of your love.

Explanation:

Accuse me thus: that I have not repaid (scanted) all your great deserts fully, and I forgot to attend (call) your dearest love, to which all bonds do tie me day by day.

That I have frequently been with unknown people (minds), and given them time, which was your own dear-purchased right; and that I have sailed my boat to all the winds, which transported me far away from your sight.

Book down both my willfulness and errors, and add therein your doubts and guess too, and frown at me for all these my faults, but shoot not me in your wakened hate (that is, take note of both my willfulness and errors, and add your doubts and guess therein, and for that frown at me if you wish, but don't hate me).

Since, my appeal says (my defense is), I did all these to prove the constancy and truthfulness (virtue) of your love.

Sonnet 118

Like as, to make our appetites more keen,
With eager compounds we our palate urge;
As, to prevent our maladies unseen,
We sicken to shun sickness, when we purge;

Even so, being full of your ne'er-cloying sweetness,
To bitter sauces did I frame my feeding,
And, sick of welfare, found a kind of meetness
To be diseased, ere that there was true needing.

Thus policy in love, to anticipate
The ills that were not, grew to faults assured,
And brought to medicine a healthful state,
Which, rank of goodness, would by ill be cured.

But thence I learn, and find the lesson true,
Drugs poison him that so fell sick of you.

Explanation:

As like, to make our appetites more keen, by taking appetizers (with eager compounds) we urge our palate (stimulate our taste); and as like, to prevent our unseen diseases (maladies) from happening, we temporarily become bit weak (sicken), when we purge (take purgative).

Even so, being full of your never-cloying (never satiated) sweetness, I did adjust my food with bitter sauces (to bitter sauces I did frame my feeding), and, being well, found a kind of feeling (meetness) of disease, of which, before that (ere that), there was true need.

Thus, in love it is a good policy to anticipate the ills that were not (i.e. ills that have not yet happened), and to take preventive medicine even though one is healthy (brought to medicine a healthful state), to prevent those anticipated ills from growing into real ills (grew to fault assured).

But thence (but from this process) I found and learned a true lesson that drug poison him who so fell sick of you (that is, from this process I found and learned a true lesson that for him who so fell sick of you (i.e. love), even drugs prove to be a poison).

Sonnet 119

What potions have I drunk of Siren tears,
Distill'd from limbecs foul as hell within,
Applying fears to hopes, and hopes to fears,
Still losing when I saw myself to win!

What wretched errors hath my heart committed,
Whilst it hath thought itself so blessed never!
How have mine eyes out of their spheres been fitted,
In the distraction of this madding fever!

O benefit of ill! Now I find true
That better is by evil still made better;
And ruin'd love, when it is built anew,
Grows fairer than at first, more strong, far greater.

So I return rebuked to my content,
And gain by ills thrice more than I have spent.

Explanation:

What poison (potions) have I drunk of Siren tears (i.e. tears of a luring, seductive and dangerous woman), distilled from a thing which is dirty within as hell, using hope for fear, and fear for hope, still losing when I saw myself wining!

What wretched errors has my heart committed, whilst it has thought itself so blessed as never before! How my eyes have been fitted out of their sphere, in the distraction of maddening fever!

O benefit of ill (i.e. O the benefit that I have gained from above ills)! Now I find that true love, which is better, is made still better by evil; and ruined love, when it is built anew, grows fairer that it was before, more strong, far greater.

So, I return to you after being rebuked (punished) to my core (content), and gain by ills thrice more than I have spent (that is, I return to you after being moved to my core by all these ill experiences, but by those ill experiences I understood the value of your true love, which is far more (three times more) valuable than what I have suffered).

Sonnet 120

That you were once unkind, befriends me now,
And for that sorrow, which I then did feel,
Needs must I under my transgression bow,
Unless my nerves were brass or hammer'd steel.

For if you were by my unkindness shaken,
As I by yours, you've passed a hell of time;
And I, a tyrant, have no leisure taken
To weight how once I suffer'd in your crime.

O, that our nights of woe might have remember'd
My deepest sense, how hard true sorrow hits,
And soon to you, as you to me, then tender'd
The humble salve which wounded bosom fits!

But that your trespass now becomes a fee;
Mine ransoms yours, and yours must ransom me.

Explanation:

The fact that you were once unkind to me, befriends me now, and for that sorrow, which I then did feel, I must bow under my sin (transgression), unless my nerves were so insensitive like brass or hammered steel.

Because, if you were shaken by my unkindness, as I by yours, you have passed a hell of time, and I, like a tyrant, have no leisure taken (i.e. not even given a thought) to weight how once I suffered in your crime.

Otherwise, that our nights of woe (nights of sorrows) might have deeply reminded me, how hard true sorrow hits, and then, immediately we both, I to you as you to me, would have tendered our wounded and humble selves to each other.

But, that your trespass (wrong) now becomes a fee; and my wrong ransoms (redeems) your wrong, and your wrong must ransoms (redeems) me.

Sonnet 121

'Tis better to be vile than vile esteemed,
When not to be receives reproach of being,
And the just pleasure lost, which is so deemed
Not by our feeling, but by others' seeing.

For why should others' false adulterate eyes
Give salutation to my sportive blood?
Or on my frailties why are frailer spies,
Which in their wills count bad what I think good?

No. - I am what I am; and they that level
At my abuses, reckon up their own:
I may be straight, though they themselves be bevel;
By their rank thoughts my deeds must not be shown;

Unless this general evil they maintain, -
All men are bad, and in their badness reign.

Explanation:

It is better to be vile (wicked) than being believed to be vile, when innocent receives reproach (blame) of being vile, the just pleasure is lost, which is so deemed not by our feeling, but by other's seeing.

For why should false adulterate (adulterous) eyes of others give salutation (i.e. bad name) to my playful spirit (sportive blood)? Or why frailer spies count my frailties (weaknesses) on their wish as bad, what I consider good?

No. - I am what I am, and they charge (level) their own abuses upon me: I may be straight, though they themselves are crocked (bevel); they should not show my deeds with their grade (rank) of thinking (by their rank thoughts my deeds must not be shown).

Unless this general evil they maintain, in their view, all man are bad, and in their badness reign (prevail).

Sonnet 122

Thy gift, thy tables, are within my brain
Full character'd with lasting memory
Which shall above that idle rank remain,
Beyond all date, even to eternity:

Or at the least so long as brain and heart
Have faculty by nature to subsist;
Till each to razed oblivion yield his part
Of thee, thy record never can be missed.

That poor retention could not so much hold,
Nor need I tallies thy dear love to score;
Therefore to give them from me was I bold,
To trust those tables that receive thee more:

To keep an adjunct to remember thee,
Were to import forgetfulness in me.

Explanation:

Your gift, your tables (papers) are within my brain fully characterized in lasting memory, which shall remain above that idle rank, beyond all date, even to eternity.

Or at least so long as the brain and heart have natural capacity to subsist: until death (razed oblivion) when each (brain and heart) lose its capacity of remembering, your record can never be missed.

That poor retention (i.e. as contained in papers etc.) could not hold so much, nor I need all that to remember (score) your dear love; therefore, I was bold to give all that from me, trusting that inner space of my heart which receives you more (to trust those tables that receive you more).

To keep something (an adjunct) to remember you, would mean importing forgetfulness in me (that is, I need nothing to keep your remembrance; your remembrance lives in my heart on its own).

Sonnet 123

No! Time, thou shalt not boast that I do change:
    Thy pyramids built up with newer might
    To me are nothing novel, nothing strange;
    They are but dressings of a former sight.

Our dates are brief, and therefore we admire
    What thou hast foist upon us that is old;
    And rather make them born to our desire,
Than think that we before have heard them told.

Thy registers and thee I both defy,
    Not wondering at the present nor the past;
    For thy records and what we see doth lie,
    And more or less by thy continual haste:

This I do vow, and this shall ever be,
I will be true, despite thy scythe and thee.

Explanation:

O Time, don't boast that I do change (i.e. O Time, don't boast that I am not unchanging): to me, your pyramids built up with new strength are nothing novel, nothing strange; they are but a new dressing of a former sight.

Our dates (i.e. human life) are brief, and therefore we admire what you have slyly presented (foist) to us which is in fact old; and rather you make us to desire them, and make us think that we have heard them told before.

O Time, I defy both you and your history (register), not wondering at the present or the past, because, your history (records) and what we see now do lie, which is made more or less by your continual haste (continual fleeting movement).

This I do vow that I will be true, and I will be true for ever, despite you and your scythe.

Sonnet 124

If my dear love were but the child of state,
It might for Fortune's bastard be unfathered,
As subject to Time's love, or to Time's hate,
Weeds among weeds, or flowers with flowers gathered.

No, it was builded far from accident;
It suffers not in smiling pomp, nor falls
Under the blow of thralled discontent,
Whereto the inviting time our fashion calls:

It fears not policy, that heretic,
Which works on leases of short-number'd hours,
But all alone stands hugely politic,
That it nor grows with heat, nor drowns with showers.

To this I witness call the fools of time,
Which die for goodness, who have lived for crime.

Explanation:

If my dear love were only the child of state (i.e. temporary whims of mind), it might be un-fathered happening for Fortune's bastard, subject to Time's love, or Time's hate, weeds among weeds, or flowers with flowers gathered.

No, it was created (builded) far from the accidental happening: it does not spoil itself (suffer) in smiling splendor (pomp), nor it bend (fall) under the blow of forced (thralled) discontent, which our present day fashion may bring about (whereto the inviting time our fashion calls).

It fears not policy, nor that heretic (religious opinion), which are based on short term standards (which works on leases of short-numbered hours), but all alone it stands hugely prudent (politic), and that it not grows with heat, nor drowns with showers.

In witness for this, I call all those, fools of time, which die for goodness, who have lived for crime.

Sonnet 125

Were it aught to me I bore the canopy,
With my extern the outward honouring,
Or laid great bases for eternity,
Which proves more short than waste or ruining?

Have I not seen dwellers on form and favour
Lose all, and more, by paying too much rent,
For compound sweet foregoing simple savour,
Pitiful thrivers, in their gazing spent?

No; - let me be obsequious in thy heart,
And take my oblation, poor but free,
Which is not mixed with seconds, knows no art,
But mutual render, only me for thee.

Hence, thou suborn'd informer! a true soul,
When most impeached, stands least in thy control.

Explanation:

Were it aught to me I bore the canopy, with my outward honouring as extern, or I aught laid great foundations (bases) for eternity, which proves more short than waste or ruining?

Have I not seen dwellers on form and favour lose all, and more, by paying too much rent, for compound sweet forgoing simple taste (savour), pitiful thrivers, in their gazing spent?

No; - let me be dutiful (obsequious) in your heart, and take you my sacrifice (oblation), poor but free, which is not mixed with inferior (seconds), knows no art (cleverness), but mutual giving (render), only me for you.

Hence, you suborned (bribed) informer, a true soul, when most impeached, would stand least in your control.

Sonnet 126

O thou, my lovely boy, who in thy power
Doth hold Time's fickle glass, his sickle, hour;
Who hast by waning grown, and therein show'st
Thy lovers withering, as thy sweet self grow'st!

If Nature, sovereign mistress over wrack,
As thou goest onwards, still will pluck thee back,
She keeps thee to this purpose, that her skill
May time disgrace, and wretched minutes kill.

Yet fear her, O thou minion of her pleasure;
She may detain, but not still keep her treasure,
Her audit, though delayed, answer'd must be,
And her quietus is to render thee.

Explanation:

O, my beloved, you does hold in your power Time's fickle (changeable) glass (mirror), Time's sickle, hour; and who has become more beauteous by growing older (who has by waning grown), and thereby making me (i.e. your lover) feel ashamed (withering), as your sweet self grows!

If nature, sovereign (supreme) mistress, destroys (over wrack) as you go onward, still it will maintain your beauty (pluck you back); she will keep you beautiful for the purpose of disgracing, and killing time's wretched power.

Yet fear her (i.e. Nature), O you favorite (minion) of her pleasure, she may postpone (detain), but will not keep her treasure (i.e. your beauty) still (in tact for ever), her audit (account), though delayed, must be answered (settled), and her quietus (silence) is for rendering (handing over) you to time.

Sonnet 127

In the old age black was not counted fair,
Or if it were, it bore not beauty's name;
But now is black beauty's successive heir,
And beauty slander'd with a bastard shame:

For since each hand hath put on nature's power,
Fairing the foul with arts' false borrow'd face,
Sweet beauty hath no name, no holy hour,
But is profaned, if not lives in disgrace.

Therefore my mistress' eyes are raven black,
Her eyes so suited, and they mourners seem
As such, who, not born fair, no beauty lack,
Slandering creation with a false esteem:

Yet so they mourn, becoming of their woe,
That every tongue say, beauty should look so.

Explanation:

In the old time (age) black was not considered as beautiful (fair), or if black really looked beautiful, it was not given beauty's name; but now black is beauty's successive heir, and the fairness (beauty) is slandered with a bastard shame.

Because, since when each one has put on natures' power by fairing the foul with make-up-art's false artificial (borrowed) face, the true sweet beauty has lost its name and right place (holy hour), and is profaned (defiled), and if not lives in disgrace.

Therefore, my love's eyes are raven black; her eyes are so suited to, and, look mournful. As such they are not born fair, yet they lack no beauty, slandering (defaming) false esteemed creation (world).

Yet, my love's eye's mournful look is so becoming that every one (tongue) say, "beauty should look like this".

Sonnet 128

How oft, when thou, my music, music play'st,
Upon that blessed wood whose motion sounds
With thy sweet fingers, when thou gently sway'st,
The wiry concord that mine ear confounds,

Do I envy those jacks, that nimble leap
To kiss the tender inward of thy hand,
Whilst my poor lips, which should that harvest reap,
At the wood's boldness by thee blushing stand!

To be so tickled, they would change their state
And situation with those dancing chips,
O'er whom thy fingers walk with gentle gait,
Making dead wood more blest than living lips.

Since saucy jacks so happy are in this,
Give them thy fingers, me thy lips to kiss.

Explanation:

How often, when you, my music, play the music upon that blessed wood (i.e. a type of harpsichord called a virginal) whose motion sounds, when with your sweet fingers you gently sway (touch), the wiry concord that pours upon my ears,

I do envy those jacks (keys) that jump quickly and easily (leap nimble) to kiss the tender inward of your hand, whilst my poor lips, which should be reaping that harvest, at the wood's (virginal's) boldness, by (beside) you blushed stand!

To be so tickled, my lips would like to change their state and situation with those dancing chips (keys), over whom your fingers walk with gentle gait, making dead wood more blest than my living lips.

Since saucy (sexy) jacks (keys) are so happy in this (i.e. by being played upon), give them your fingers, and give me your lips to kiss.

Sonnet 129

The expense of spirit in a waste of shame
Is lust in action; and till action, lust
Is perjured, murderous, bloody, full of blame,
Savage, extreme, rude, cruel, not to trust;

Enjoyed no sooner, but despised straight;
Past reason hunted; and no sooner had,
Past reason hated, as a swallow'd bait,
On purpose laid to make the taker mad:

Mad in pursuit, and in possession so;
Had, having, and in quest to have extreme;
A bliss in proof, - and prov'd, a very woe;
Before, a joy proposed; behind a dream:

All this the world well knows; yet none knows well
To shun the heaven that leads men to this hell.

Explanation:

The lust in action is the loss (expense) of spirit in a waste of shame; and till action (i.e. till put in action) lust is perjured, murderous, bloody, full of shame, savage, extreme, rude, cruel, not worthy of trust.

Enjoyed no sooner, but despised straight (immediately); it arises immediately on hunting the past reason; but its past reason is hated as swallowed bait (lure), which is laid (planted) on purpose to make the taker mad.

Its pursuit is mad, and its possession is also mad; had (i.e. its past enjoyment), having (i.e. its current enjoyment), and the quest (search) to have it in extreme - all these three seems a sure bliss, but in fact proves a very woe (misery), first it seems like a proposal for joy, but in fact happens to be dream (unreal).

All (world) knows this well, but no one knows well how to keep away from this heaven that leads men to the hell (that is, all knows well that lust is bad, but no one knows well how to keep away from its lure, which feels like heaven when having, but afterwards leads men to hell).

Sonnet 130

My Mistress' eyes are nothing like the sun;
Coral is far more red than her lips' red:
If snow be white, why then her breasts are dun;
If hairs be wires, black wires grown on her head.

I have seen roses damask'd, red and white,
But no such roses see I in her cheeks;
And in some perfumes is there more delight
Than in the breath that from my Mistress reeks.

I love to hear her speak, - yet well I know
That music hath a far more pleasing sound;
I grant I never saw a goddess go, -
My Mistress when she walks, treads on the ground;

And yet, by heaven, I think my love as rare
As any she belied with false compare.

Explanation:

My love's (my Mistress's) eyes are not bright as like sun; coral is far more red than her lips' redness; her breasts are dun (greyish-brown) but are not like snow white; and her hairs are ordinary hairs but are not like golden wires.

I have seen red and white damasked roses (i.e. very fragrant cultivated roses), but there is no such roses in her cheeks; and in some perfumes there is more delight than the smell of my love's breath.

I do love to hear her speak, yet I know very well that the music has far more pleasing sound than her voice; I grant that when my love walks she walks well on the ground, but I have never saw in her a goddess walking.

And yet, by heaven (i.e. by swear of heaven), I think my love is as rare as any that she belied with false compare (that is, and yet, by heaven, I think that my love is as rare & precious as all above things falsely compared with her - like sun, snow-whiteness, rose, perfume, music, goddess, etc.).

Sonnet 131

Thou art as tyrannous, so as thou art,
As those whose beauties proudly make them cruel;
For well thou know'st to my dear doting heart
Thou art the fairest and most precious jewel,

Yet, in good faith, some say that thee behold,
Thy face hath not the power to make love groan:
To say they err, I dare not be so bold,
Although I swear it to myself alone,

And, to be sure that is not false I swear,
A thousand groans, but thinking on thy face,
One on another's neck, do witness bear
Thy black is fairest in my judgment's place.

In nothing art thou black, save in thy deeds,
And thence this slander, as I think, proceeds.

Explanation:

Such as you are, you are tyrannous (tyrannical), like those whose beauties make them cruel. You know well that to my dear doting (blindly loving) heart you are the fairest and most precious jewel.

Yet, some who see (behold) you, say in good faith that your face has not the power to make men sigh. I dare not be so bold to say that they are wrong (err), although I swear it to myself alone that your face does have that power.

And, to be sure that it is not false I swear, that just thinking on your face brings me a thousand sigh, and when we are close (one on another's neck), it does witness that your black is the fairest in my judgment.

You are black in nothing save (except) in your reprehensible behavior (deeds), and from which, I think, this slander (i.e. criticism about you) proceeds.

Sonnet 132

Thine eyes I love, and they, as pitying me,
Knowing thy heart torments me with disdain,
Have put on black, and loving mourners be,
Looking with pretty ruth upon my pain.

And truly not the morning sun of heaven
Better becomes the grey cheeks of the east,
Nor that full star that ushers in the even
Doth half that glory to the sober west,

As those two mourning eyes become thy face:
O, let it then as well beseem thy heart
To mourn for me, since mourning doth thee grace,
And suit thy pity like in every part.

Then will I swear beauty herself is black,
And all they foul that thy complexion lack.

Explanation:

I love your eyes, and they, knowing that your heart torments me with disdain (scorn), have put on black, as pitying me like loving mourners, and are looking with pretty ruth (sorrow) upon my pain.

And truly, not the morning sun of heaven better becomes (suits) the grey cheeks of the east, nor that full star that ushers in the evening (evening star) does half that glory to the sober west, as those two mourning eyes become (suit) your face.

O, let then your heart also mourn for me (let then mourn for me as well beseem your heart), since mourning does grace you, and it suits your pity like in every part.

Then I will swear that the beauty herself is black, and all those who lack your complexion (color) are ugly (that is, if your heart also mourn for me, then I will swear that beauty herself is black, blackness is the essential nature of the beauty, and all those who are not black are ugly)!

Sonnet 133

Beshrew that heart that makes my heart to groan
For that deep wound it gives my friend and me!
Is't not enough to torture me alone,
But slave to slavery my sweet'st friend must be?

Me from myself thy cruel eye hath taken,
And my next self thou harder hast engross'd,
Of him, myself, and thee, I am forsaken;
A torment thrice three-fold thus to be crossed.

Prison my heart in thy steel bosom's ward,
But then my friend's heart let my poor heart bail;
Who e'er keeps me, let my heart be his guard;
Thou canst not then use rigour in my gaol:

And yet thou wilt; for I, being pent in thee
Perforce am thine, and all that is in me.

Explanation:

Beshrew (curse) your heart that makes my heart to groan for that deep wound it gives to my friend and me! Is it not enough to torture me alone, that you made my sweetest friend slave to slavery?

Your cruel eye has taken me from myself, and you harder have engrossed (monopolized) my next self (i.e. my best friend); I am forsaken by myself, by my best friend, and by you; and thus three-fold torment (anguish) is thwarted (crossed) thrice upon me.

Do imprison my heart in your steel bosom's ward (jail), but then let my poor heart bail (release) my friend's heart from you; whoever keeps me, but let my heart be my friend's guard, so that you can not use harshness (rigour) upon my friend, who is in my shelter (gaol).

And, I know, yet you will use rigour; because I, being confined (pent) in you, me and all that is dwelling in me, is necessarily (perforce) yours.

Sonnet 134

So now I have confess'd that he is thine,
And I myself am mortgag'd to thy will;
Myself I'll forfeit, so that other mine
Thou wilt restore, to be my comfort still:

But thou wilt not, nor he will not be free,
For thou art covetous, and he is kind;
He learn'd but, surety-like, to write for me,
Under that bond that him as fast doth bind.

The statute of thy beauty thou wilt take,
Thou usurer, that putt'st forth all to use,
And sue a friend, came debtor for my sake;
So him I lose through my unkind abuse.

Him have I lost; thou hast both him and me;
He pays the whole, and yet am I not free.

Explanation:

So now I have confessed that he (i.e. my friend) is yours, and I myself am mortgaged (surrendered) to your will (command); I will forfeit (i.e. give up voluntarily) myself, so that you will restore my friend (other mine), for my comfort's sake.

But you will not free him, nor he will want to be free, because you are covetous (greedy), and he is kind; he knew that, but to be my surety, he signed (write) for me under that bond, which does bind him too as fast.

I know, the due (statute) of your beauty you will take, you usurer (usurer is one who lends money at exorbitantly high rate of interest), you will do everything possible (you put forth all to use), and will sue my friend, who became your debtor for my sake; and thus (so) I lost him because of my this unkind abuse (i.e. because of unkindly making him my surety).

I have lost my friend, and now you have both, my friend and me; he pays the whole, and yet I am not free (i.e. debt-free).

Sonnet 135

Whoever hath her wish, thou hast thy will,
And will to boot, and will in over-plus;
More than enough am I that vex thee still,
To thy sweet will making addition thus.

Wilt thou, whose will is large and spacious,
Not once vouchsafe to hide my will in thine?
Shall will in others seem right gracious,
And in my will no fair acceptance shine?

The sea, all water, yet receives rain still,
And in abundance addeth to his store;
So thou, being rich in will, add to thy will
One will of mine, to make thy large will more.

Let no unkind, no fair beseechers kill;
Think all but one, and me in that one Will.

Explanation:

Whoever has desire (wish) for her, you have your approval (will), the will in addition (to boot), and the will in full (over-plus); I bother (vex) you by saying that there is more than enough in me, to make thus addition in your sweet will.

Shall not you, whose will is large and spacious, once graciously consent (vouchsafe) to fulfill my will voluntarily (hide my will in your will)? Why the will of others seem right gracious to you, and why do not shine your fair acceptance for my will?

The sea is all water, yet it receives rain still, and adds in abundance to its store, so you, being rich in will, add one will of mine to your will, and make your large will still more large.

Don't refuse (kill) the will of his, who is not unkind, and who fairly seeks (fair beseecher); you do fulfill will of all (think all) but one, and that one (i.e. unfulfilled) will is mine!

Sonnet 136

If thy soul check thee that I come so near,
Swear to thy blind soul that I was thy Will,
And will, thy soul knows, is admitted there;
Thus far for love, my love-suit, sweet, fulfil.

Will will fulfill the treasure of thy love,
Ay, fill it full with wills, and my will one,
In things of great receipt with ease we prove;
Among a number one is reckon'd none.

Then in the number let me pass untold,
Though in thy stores' account one must be;
For nothing hold me, so it please thee hold
That nothing me, a something sweet to thee;

Make but my name thy love, and love that still,
And then thou lovest me, - for my name is Will.

Explanation:

If your soul restrain (check) you, saying that I came so near to you, then swear to your blind soul that I am your *Will* (i.e. your William Shakespeare), and your soul knows that Will is admitted there; thus far, for love my love-suit (i.e. courtship) is sweetly fulfilled.

Will will fulfill the treasure of your love, ay, fill it full with wills (i.e. with many desires), and with ease we prove that in things of great receipt (capacity) my will is one (unified); as, among those no one is reckoned as a number one.

Then let me pass uncounted (untold) in the calculation (number), though one must be in your store's account; because nothing holds me, so please you hold it, that nothing me, which is a something sweet to you.

Make your love but (only in) my name, and still love that love, and then it would mean that you love me, - because my name is *Will* (i.e. William Shakespeare).

Sonnet 137

Thou blind fool, Love, what dost thou to mine eyes,
   That they behold, and see not what they see?
   They know what beauty is, see where it lies,
   Yet what the best is, take the worst to be.

If eyes, corrupt by over-partial looks,
   Be anchor'd in the bay where all men ride,
   Why of eyes' falsehood hast thou forged hooks,
   Where to the judgment of my heart is tied?

Why should my heart think that a several plot,
   Which my heart knows the wide world's commonplace?
   Or mine eyes, seeing this, say this is not,
   To put fair truth upon so foul a face?

In things right true my heart and eyes have err'd,
   And to this false plague are they now transferr'd.

Explanation:

O you blind fool, Love, what you did to mine eyes that they behold, but see (notice) not what they see? They know what the beauty is, and see where it lies, yet they take as the worst, what in fact the best is.

If eyes, corrupt by over-partiality for someone's looks, are anchored (fixed) in the bay where all men ride, why you have made the eye's such falsehood a forged hook, to which judgment of my heart is tied? (That is, if eyes, being over-fond for someone's looks, are fixed therein, then why you made such eye's false report as standard on the basis of which my heart's judgment becomes biased?).

Why should my heart think something a several (i.e. private, my own) plot, which, my heart knows, is the wide world's commonplace (public property)? Or why mine eyes, even after seeing this, say that this is not public property, to put high value (fair truth) upon so disgusting (foul) face?

My heart and eyes have erred in connection with the right true things, and they (i.e. my heart and eyes) are now transferred to this false plague (fever).

Sonnet 138

When my love swears that she is made of truth,
I do believe her, though I know she lies;
That she might think me some untutor'd youth,
Unlearned in the world's false subtleties.

Thus vainly thinking that she thinks me young,
Although she knows my days are past the best,
Simply I credit her false-speaking tongue;
On both sides thus is simple truth supprest,

But wherefore says she not she is unjust?
And wherefore say not I that I am old?
O, loves best habit is in seeming trust,
And age in love loves not to have years told:

Therefore I lie with her, and she with me,
And in our faults by lies we flatter'd be.

Explanation:

When she swears that she is made of truth (i.e. that she is telling truth), I do believe her, though I know she lies; she might be thinking me some uneducated (untutored) youth, unaware (unlearned) in the false subtleties of the world.

Thus vainly (conceitedly) thinking that she thinks me young, although she knows that my best days (i.e. youthful days) have already passed, simply I believe (credit) her false-speaking tongue: thus on both sides the simple truth is suppressed.

But for what she does not say she is unjust? And for what I do not say I am old? O, loves best habit (dressing) is in seeming trust, and the aged one, who is in love, don't like to have his years told (and age in love loves not to have years told).

Therefore, I lie with her, and she lies with me, and we both feel flattered by lies in our faults.

Sonnet 139

O, call not me to justify the wrong
That thy unkindness lays upon my heart;
Wound me not with thine eye, but with thy tongue;
Use power with power, and slay me not by art.

Tell me thou lov'st elsewhere: but in my sight,
Dear heart, forbear to glance thine eye aside.
What need'st thou wound with cunning, when thy might
Is more than my o'er press'd defence can 'bide?

Let me excuse thee: ah! my love well knows
Her pretty looks have been mine enemies;
And therefore from my face she turns my foes,
That they elsewhere might dart their injuries:

Yet do not so: but since I am near slain,
Kill me outright, with looks, and rid my pain.

Explanation:

O, don't call me to justify the wrong that your unkindness inflicts (lays) upon my heart; don't wound me with your eye, but would me with your tongue: use the power forcefully (with power), but don't slay (kill) me with trick (art).

Tell me that you love someone else: but in my sight (presence), dear heart, avoid (forbear) to glance your eye aside. What makes you need to wound me with cunning (trick), when your might (strength) is more than what my over pressed defence can endure?

Let me excuse (forgive) you: ah! my love knows well that her pretty looks have been my enemies, and therefore, she turns my foes (i.e. her eyes) away from my face, so that they might dart (inflict) there injuries elsewhere.

Yet don't do so: since I am near (almost) slain, kill me outright (fully), with looks, and free (rid) me from my pain.

Sonnet 140

Be wise as thou art cruel; do not press
My tongue-tied patience with too much disdain;
Lest sorrow lends me words, and words express
The manner of my pity-wanting pain.

If I might teach thee wit, better it were,
Though not to love, yet, love, to tell me so;
(As testy sick men, when their deaths be near,
No news but health from their physicians know;)

For, if I should despair, I should grow mad,
And in my madness might speak ill of thee:
Now this ill-wresting world is grown so bad,
Mad slanderers by mad ears believed be.

That I may not be so, nor thou belied,
Bear thine eyes straight, though thy proud heart go wide.

Explanation:

Be wise as you are cruel; and do not strain (press) my tongue-tied (silent) patience with too much disdain (scorn), otherwise, my sorrow would lend me words, and those words would express in the manner in which pity-wanting pain expresses.

If I were to teach you cleverness (wit), better it would be, "Though you do not love me, yet, my love, tell me that you do love me". (I am telling this as like testy (irritable) sick men, whose death is near, and who want to hear no news from their physicians except the news of their good health).

Because, if I despair (i.e. if I be without hope), I would grow mad, and in my madness might speak ill of you; and as now this ill-wrestling world is grown so bad, that the mad ears of mad slanderers would believe it as true.

So, in order not to make me so (i.e. mad speaking ill), nor you be belied, keep (bear) your eyes straight, though your proud heart go wide (that is, even if there is no love for me in your proud heart, then also pretend to keep your eyes straight, and not wondering upon someone else, so that I do not become mad, and belie you by speaking ill of you).

Sonnet 141

In faith I do not love thee with mine eyes,
For they in thee a thousand errors note;
But 'tis my heart that loves what they despise,
Who in despite of view is pleased to dote.

Nor are mine ears with thy tongue's tune delighted:
Nor tender feeling, to base touches prone,
Nor taste nor smell, desire to be invited
To any sensual feast with thee alone:

But my five wits, nor my five senses can
Dissuade one foolish heart from serving thee,
Who leaves unswayed the likeness of a man,
Thy proud heart's slave and vassal wretch to be;

Only my plague thus far I count my gain,
That she that makes me sin, awards me pain.

Explanation:

In truth, I do not love you with my eyes, for they note (see) in you a thousand errors; but it is my heart that loves what my eyes despise (hate), despite of seeing your errors my heart is pleased to dote (blindly love).

Nor my ears are delighted with your tongue's sound (tune); neither my tender feeling of touch, prone to base touches, nor my taste, nor my smell desire to be invited to any sensual feast (sensual enjoyment) with you alone.

But neither my five wits (i.e. five minds*), nor my five senses (i.e. hearing, touch, sight, taste and smell) can dissuade my one foolish heart from serving you, who leaves me without any self-control (unswayed), and makes me (likeness of man) your proud heart's slave and wretched (miserable) vassal.

So far, only thing that I can count as gain is my plague (fever), and that she, who makes me sin, awards (gives) me pain.

(*As per G. I. Gurdjieff's 4th Way Teaching, each human being has five minds, viz, intellectual, emotional, instinctive, moving and sex; and each of them have separate function of its own in human psyche)

Sonnet 142

Love is my sin, and thy dear virtue hate,
Hate of my sin, grounded on sinful loving:
O, but with mine compare thou thine own state,
And thou shalt find it merits not reproving;

Or, if it do, not from those lips of thine,
That have profaned their scarlet ornaments,
And sealed false bonds of love as oft as mine;
Robbed others' beds' revenues of their rents.

Be it lawful I love thee, as thou lovest those
Whom thine eyes woo as mine importune thee:
Root pity in thy heart, that, when it grows,
Thy pity may deserve to pitied be.

If thou dost seek to have what thou dost hide,
By self-example mayst thou be denied!

Explanation:

Love is my sin, and hate is your dear virtue, and your hate for my sin (love) is grounded on sinful loving; O, but you compare your own state with mine, and you will find that my state does not merit reproving (refusal).

Or, if it really does merit reproving, then also not from those your lips, that have profaned (spoiled, defiled) their own bright redness (scarlet ornament), by locking themselves with others' lips in false love affairs (sealed false bonds of love) as often as mine; and have unlawfully enjoyed the beds of others (robbed others' beds' revenues of their rent).

Be it lawful I love you, as you love those whom your eyes woo (court) as my eyes importune (repeatedly urge) you: root (implant) pity in your heart, so that, when it grows, your heart and your pity may become worthy of pitying.

If you do seek to have what you do not give (hide), then by self-example you may be denied that (that is, if you seek love from others but you yourself do not give your love, then by your own self-example, love would be denied to you)!

Sonnet 143

Lo, as a careful housewife runs to catch
One of her feather'd creatures broke away,
Sets down her babe, and makes all swift dispatch
In pursuit of the thing she would have stay;

Whilst her neglected child holds her in chase,
Cries to catch her whose busy care is bent
To follow that which flies before her face,
Not prizing her poor infant's discontent;

So runn'st thou after that which flies from thee,
Whilst I thy babe chase thee afar behind;
But if thou catch thy hope, turn back to me,
And play the mother's part, kiss me, be kind:

So will I pray that thou mayst have thy Will
If thou turn back, and my loud crying still.

Explanation:

Lo, as like a careful housewife runs to catch one of her pet bird (feathered creature) broke away, sets down her babe, and run with all her swift in pursuit of the that thing (i.e. bird) which she like to keep with her;

Whilst her neglected (set down) child chases after her, cries to catch her whose attention (care) is busy in following that (i.e. bird) which flies before her face, not valuing (prizing) her poor infant's discontent (dissatisfaction);

So run you after that which flies from you, whilst I thy babe chase you afar behind, but if you catch your hope (i.e. that which you chase), then turn back to me, and play mother's role, kiss me, be kind.

If you turn back and still (i.e. appease) my loud crying, I will so pray that you may have your *Will* (i.e. if you turn back and appease my loud crying, then I will so pray that you may have that which you desire).

Sonnet 144

Two loves I have of comfort and despair,
Which like two spirits do suggest me still;
The better angel is a man right fair,
The worser spirit a woman, colour'd ill,

To win me soon to hell, my female evil
Tempteth my better angel from my side,
And would corrupt my saint to be a devil,
Wooing his purity with her foul pride.

And whether that my angel be turn'd fiend,
Suspect I may, yet not directly tell;
But, being both from me, both to each friend,
I guess one angel in another's hell.

Yet this shall I ne'er know, but live in doubt,
Till my bad angel fire my good one out.

Explanation:

I have two loves; one of comfort and another of despair, which like two spirits do influence (suggest) me still; the better angel is a right fair man, and the worser spirit is an ill colored woman.

To win me soon to hell, my female evil tempts my better angel from my side, and would corrupt my saint (fair angel) to be a devil, by wooing his purity with her disgusting (foul) pride.

Whether that my fair angel is turned into Satan (fiend), I may suspect, yet I can not directly tell; but, being both from me, both are friends to each-other, and I guess one angel is in another's hell.

Yet, this I shall never know, but would live in doubt, till my bad angel fire (drive) my good angel out.

Sonnet 145

Those lips that Love's own hand did make
Breathed forth the sound that said, "I hate,"
To me that languished for her sake:
But when she saw my woeful state,

Straight in her heart did mercy come,
Chiding that tongue, that ever sweet
Was used in giving gentle doom;
And taught it thus anew to greet:

"I hate" she altered with an end,
That follow'd it as gentle day
Doth follow night, who like a fiend
From heaven to hell is flown away.

"I hate" from hate away she threw,
And saved my life, saying, "not you."

Explanation:

Those lips that love's own hand did make breathed forth (uttered) the sound that said, "I hate". That sound languished (pined) me for her sake, but when she saw my woeful (miserable) state,

The mercy did come straight in her heart, chiding (rebuking) that ever sweet tongue which was used in giving gentle doom (i.e. slow death), and thus taught it anew to greet:

She altered the phrase "I hate" by adding at an end, that followed it as gentle day do follow night, who like a fiend (Satan) flown away from heaven to hell.

She threw away hate from "I hate", and saved my life by saying, "not you".

Sonnet 146

Poor soul, the centre of my sinful earth,
Fool'd by these rebel powers that thee array,
Why dost thou pine within, and suffer dearth,
Painting thy outward walls so costly gay?

Why so large cost, having so short a lease,
Dost thou upon thy fading mansion spend?
Shall worms, inheritors of this excess,
Eat up thy charge? Is this thy body's end?

Then, soul, live thou upon thy servant's loss,
And let that pine to aggravate thy store;
Buy terms divine in selling hours of dross;
Within be fed, without be rich no more:

So shalt thou feed on Death, that feeds on men,
And, death once dead, there's no more dying then.

Explanation:

O poor soul, the center of my sinful body (earth), fooled by these rebel powers that you array (arrange in a pleasing way), why do you pine within, and suffer dearth (lack), by painting your outward walls (body) so costly gay?

Why do you spend so large cost upon your fading mansion (dwelling place – body), having so short a lease (life)? Shall worms, inheritors of this excess (i.e. residue of body) eat up your charge? Is only this your body's end?

Then, soul, live upon (i.e. transform) your servant's loss (i.e. body's suffering), and let your body pine to add (aggravate) to your richness (store); buy divine terms by selling hours of dross (i.e. use efforts of body for earning divine worth), be fed within, without be rich no more (i.e. don't try to ornament the body from outside any more).

This way you shall feed on Death, which feeds on men, and, once death is dead, then there is no more dying (that is, by willingly accepting, absorbing & transforming sufferings that life may inflict, you shall feed on death, which feeds on men, and, once you have transformed the fear of death (- that would be the death of Death), then there is no more dying).

Sonnet 147

My love is as a fever, longing still
For that which longer nurseth the disease;
Feeding on that which doth preserve the ill,
The uncertain sickly appetite to please.

My reason, the physician to my love,
Angry that his prescriptions are not kept,
Hath left me, and I desperate now approve
Desire is death, which physic did except.

Past cure I am, now reason is past care,
And frantic mad with evermore unrest;
My thoughts and my discourse as mad men's are,
At random from the truth vainly expressed;

For I have sworn thee fair, and thought thee bright,
Who art as black as hell, as dark as night.

Explanation:

My love for you is like a fever, still longing for that which longer nurses (prolongs) the disease; feeding on that which does preserve the illness, and pleases the uncertain sickly appetite.

My reason (wisdom), the physician to my love (disease), who is angry that his prescriptions (instructions) are not kept (carried out), has left me, and in desperation now I agree (approve) that the desire, which physic did forbid (except), is death.

Now I am past (beyond) cure, and my reason is past (beyond) care, and is frantic mad with evermore unrest; my thoughts and my utterance (discourse) are like that of mad men, vainly expressing from the truth at random.

Because, I have sworn you fair, and thought you bright, who, in fact, are as black as hell, and as dark as night.

Sonnet 148

O me! what eyes hath love put in my head,
Which have no correspondence with true sight!
Or, if they have, where is my judgement fled,
That censures falsely what they see aright?

If that be fair whereon my false eyes dote,
What means the world to say it is not so?
If it be not, then love doth well denote
Love's eye is not so true as all men's: no,

How can it? O how can Love's eye be true,
That is so vexed with watching and with tears?
No marvel then though I mistake my view;
The sun itself sees not till heaven clears.

O cunning Love! with tears thou keepst me blind,
Lest eyes well-seeing thy foul faults should find.

Explanation:

O me! What kind of eyes love has put in my head, which have no correspondence with true sight (that is, what my eyes see has no correspondence with actual sight)! Or, if they have, then, where my judgement has fled, that it censures (condemns) falsely what they see aright (correctly)?

If that is fair which my false eyes dote (blindly love), then, why the world say it is not fair? If it is not, then love does denote (indicate) well that love's eye is not so true as all men's are:

No, how it can be? O how can love's eye be true (clear), which is so distressed (vexed) with keeping watch (watching) and with weeping (tears)? Then there is no marvel that sun itself can not see clearly till heaven clears (clouds clear), though I may mistake my view.

O cunning Love, you keep me blind with tears, otherwise eyes being capable of seeing well (well-seeing) should find your foul (disgusting) faults.

Sonnet 149

Canst thou, O cruel! say I love thee not,
When I, against myself, with thee partake?
Do I not think on thee, when I forgot
Am of myself, all tyrant, for thy sake?

Who hateth thee that I do call my friend?
On whom frown'st thou that I do fawn upon?
Nay if thou low'rst on me, do I not spend
Revenge upon myself with present moan?

What merit do I myself respect,
That is so proud thy service to despise,
When all my best doth worship thy defect,
Commanded by the motion of thine eyes?

But, love, hate on, for now I know thy mind;
Those that can see thou lov'st, and I am blind.

Explanation:

O cruel, can you say that I don't love you, when I, against myself, partake (share) with you? Do I not think on you, when I, all tyrant, am forgot of myself for your sake?

Who hates you that I do call my friend? Who I flatter (fawn) on whom you frown? Nay, if you lower (frown) on me, do I not take (spend) revenge upon myself with this present moan?

Which merit do I myself respect, that is so proud to despise (hate) your service, when all my best do worship your defects, commanded by the motion of your eyes?

But, Love, hate on (continue hating), for now I know your mind; you love those who can see, and I am blind (that is, but, love, continue hating me, as, now I know that you love only those who can see your faults, and I am blind towards your faults).

Sonnet 150

O, from what power hast thou this powerful might,
With insufficiency my heart to sway?
To make me give the lie to my true sight,
And swear that brightness doth not grace the day?

Whence hast thou this becoming of things ill,
That in the very refuse of thy deeds
There is such strength and warrantise of skill,
That in my mind, thy worst all best exceeds?

Who taught thee how to make me love thee more,
The more I hear and see just cause of hate?
O, though I love what others do abhor,
With others thou shouldst not abhor my state;

If thy unworthiness raised love in me,
More worthy I to be beloved of thee.

Explanation:

O, from what power do you have this mighty strength, that even with shortcomings (insufficiency) you sway my heart, and make me disbelieve that which I really see (make me give lie to my true sight), and make me swear that brightness does not grace the day?

From where you have this becoming of ill things (i.e. that even ill things look becoming), and that in the very act of yours (in the very refuse of your deeds) there is such strength and guarantee of skill that, in my mind, your worst deed seem excelling than all best deeds?

Who taught you how to make me love you more, when more I hear and see the just cause for hating you? O, though I love what (i.e. you whom) others do abhor (hate), but with others you should not abhor (hate) my state.

If your unworthiness has raised love in me, then more worthy I am to be beloved of yours.

Sonnet 151

Love is too young to know what conscience is:
Yet who knows not, conscience is born of love?
Then, gentle cheater, urge not my amiss,
Lest guilty of my faults thy sweet self prove.

For thou betraying me, I do betray
My nobler part to my gross body's treason;
My soul doth tell my body that he may
Triumph in love; flesh stays no further reason;

But, rising at thy name, doth point out thee,
As his triumphant prize. Proud of this pride,
He is contented thy poor drudge to be,
To stand in thy affairs, fall by thy side,

No want of conscience hold it that I call
Her "love," for whose dear love I rise and fall.

Explanation:

Love is too young to know what conscience is, yet who don't know that the conscience is born of love? Then, gentle cheater, don't urge my amiss (wrong), otherwise your sweet self shall prove guilty of my faults.

For, you betraying me, I do betray my nobler part to my gross body's treason (treachery), though my soul does tell my body that he may triumph in love; flesh (body) stays no further reason;

But, rising at your name does point out you as his triumphant prize. Being proud of this pride, he is contended to be your poor drudge (slave), to stand in your affair, and to fall by your side.

No want of conscience I hold that which I call her "love", for whose dear love I rise and fall.

Sonnet 152

In loving thee thou know'st I am forsworn,
But thou art twice forsworn, to me love swearing;
In act thy bed-vow broke, and new faith torn,
In vowing new hate after new love bearing.

But why of two oaths' breach do I accuse thee,
When I break twenty? I am perjured most;
For all my vows are oaths but to misuse thee,
And all my honest faith in thee is lost:

For I have sworn deep oaths of thy deep kindness,
Oaths of thy love, thy truth, thy constancy;
And, to enlighten thee, gave eyes to blindness,
Or made them swear against the thing they see;

For I have sworn thee fair: more perjured I,
To swear, against the truth, so foul a lie!

Explanation:

You know that in loving you I am forsworn (perjured), but in swearing love to me you are twice forsworn; you broke your bed-vow (i.e. vow of not sleeping with others), and you have torn new faith, in vowing new hate after bearing new love-affair.

But why for two oaths' breach do I accuse you when I break twenty? I am perjured most, as, all my vows are oaths only to misuse you, and all my honest faith in you is lost.

Because, I have sworn deep oaths of your deep kindness, oaths of your love, your truth, your constancy, and moreover, to enlighten you, I gave my eyes to blindness, or made my eyes swear not to see faults in you (or made them swear against the thing they see).

Because I have sworn you fair, I am more perjured, as, to swear, against the truth, on so foul (disgusting) a lie.

Sonnet 153

Cupid lay by his brand, and fell asleep:
A maid of Dian's this advantage found,
And his love-kindling fire did quickly steep
In a cold valley-fountain of that ground;

Which borrow'd from this holy fire of love
A dateless lively heat, still to endure,
And grew a seething bath, which yet men prove
Against strange maladies a sovereign cure.

But at my mistress' eye Love's brand new-fired,
The boy for trial needs would touch my breast;
I, sick withal, the help of bath desired,
And thither hied, a sad distempered guest,

But found no cure: the bath for my help lies
Where Cupid got new fire, - my mistress' eyes.

Explanation:

Cupid lay by his brand (i.e. Love-bow), and fall asleep: a maid of Dian's has found this opportunity, and quickly steeped its love-kindling-fire in a cold valley-fountain of that ground.

That valley-fountain borrowed from this holy fire of love a dateless, still enduring, lively heat and grew into a seething bath, which yet proves a sovereign cure against strange maladies (diseases).

But Cupid's Love-bow (love's brand) fired anew at my lover's (mistress') eye, the boy (i.e. Cupid) for trial needs touched my breast; and I, sick with that touch (withal), desiring the help of bath, hastened towards that valley-fountain (thither hied), in a sad distempered quest.

But I found no cure: the bath in that valley-fountain could not help me, where Cupid got new fire, - my lover's eyes (that is, my lover's eyes are so love-full that even Cupid gets new fire from there, and then, even the bath in valley-fountain could not cure my love-fever).

Sonnet 154

The little love-god, lying once asleep
Laid by his side his heart-inflaming brand,
Whilst many nymphs that vow'd chaste life to keep
Came tripping by; but in her maiden hand

The fairest votary took up that fire
Which many legions of true hearts had warmed:
And so the general of hot desire
Was sleeping by a virgin hand disarm'd.

This brand she quenched in a cool well by,
Which from Love's fire took heat perpetual,
Growing a bath and healthful remedy
For men diseas'd; but I, my mistress' thrall,

Came there for cure, and this by that I prove,
Love's fire heats water, water cools not love.

Explanation:

The little love-god (i.e. Cupid) was once lying asleep, laying his heart-inflaming brand (i.e. love-bow) by his side, whilst many nymphs (spring goddesses) that vowed to keep life chaste came tripping by;

The fairest votary (goddess) took up in her maiden hand that fire which had warmed many legions of true hearts: and thus the general of hot fire (i.e. Cupid) was disarmed by a virgin hand when he was sleeping.

She quenched (extinguished) this brand (i.e. Love-bow) in a nearby cool well, which took perpetual heat from Love's fire, and grown into a bath of healthful remedy for diseased men;

But I, my lover's slave (mistress's thrall), went there for cure, and by this (i.e. by my this experience) I prove that love's fire heats water, but water do not cool love (that is, even the bath in that well could not cure me from my love-fever, so, by my this experience, I prove that love's fire heats water, but water do not cool love).

Printed in Great
Britain
by Amazon